Science in
Theology

Science in Theology

Encounters between Science and the Christian Tradition

Neil Messer

t&tclark

LONDON • NEW YORK • OXFORD • NEW DELHI • SYDNEY

T&T CLARK
Bloomsbury Publishing Plc
50 Bedford Square, London, WC1B 3DP, UK
1385 Broadway, New York, NY 10018, USA

BLOOMSBURY, T&T CLARK and the T&T Clark logo are trademarks of
Bloomsbury Publishing Plc

First published in Great Britain 2020

Cover design: Terry Woodley
Cover image © Moon installation in Ely Cathedral, Cambridgeshire by UK artist
Luke Jerram. Geoffrey Robinson/Alamy Stock Photo.

A catalogue record for this book is available from the British Library.

A catalog record for this book is available from the Library of Congress.

ISBN: HB: 978-0-5676-8982-5
PB: 978-0-5676-8981-8
ePDF: 978-0-5676-8983-2
ePUB: 978-0-5676-8984-9

Typeset by Deanta Global Publishing Services, Chennai, India

To find out more about our authors and books visit www.bloomsbury.com
and sign up for our newsletters.

In memoriam
David Protheroe (D. P.) Davies
19 July 1939–6 September 2019

CONTENTS

ACKNOWLEDGEMENTS

This book has its origins in a conversation with Bethany Sollereder at the 2016 annual conference of the Science and Religion Forum in Birmingham, UK. I am grateful to Bethany for encouraging me to write the book and for her help with the funding application that supported it. Thanks also to colleagues at the University of Winchester for their assistance with the arrangements that freed me to do the work.

At various stages, conversations with Chris Southgate and Louise Hickman, and comments from several anonymous reviewers, were very valuable in clarifying the shape and focus of the book and highlighting important issues to address. Some of the material in Chapter 4 was presented at the seventeenth European Conference on Science and Theology, Lyon, France, April 2018, which provided an opportunity for helpful discussion. Chris Southgate, Gunnar Innerdal and Robbie Mackenzie kindly read and commented on complete or partial drafts of the book. I am most grateful for the advice I received in all these ways, though of course I remain responsible for whatever I have failed to learn from it.

My thanks to Anna Turton, Sarah Blake, Veerle Van Steenhuyse and their colleagues at Bloomsbury for supporting this project so enthusiastically and for their help with the publication process. And heartfelt thanks as always to Janet, Fiona and Rowan for the love and support that take so many different forms.

This project was made possible through the support of a grant from Templeton World Charity Foundation, Inc. The opinions expressed in this publication are those of the author and do not necessarily reflect the views of Templeton World Charity Foundation, Inc.

An earlier and shorter version of Chapter 3 was published as Neil Messer, 'Evolution and Theodicy: How (Not) to Do Science and Theology', *Zygon: Journal of Religion and Science*, 53.3 (2018), pp. 821–35, copyright by the Joint Publication Board of Zygon. Permission to reuse this material is gratefully acknowledged. Some material from Chapters 1 and 2 was used in Neil Messer, 'Theologie und Naturwissenschaft. Neue Wege der Begegnung von Theologie und Naturwissenschaften', *Ökumenische Rundschau*, 69.1 (2020). I am grateful to the editors and publishers of *Ökumenische Rundschau* for allowing me to retain the copyright of this article.

Christopher Southgate's poems 'Knowing' and 'Crick, Watson, and the Double Helix', quoted on pp. 157 and 161, are from Christopher Southgate, *Easing the Gravity Field: Poems of Science and Love* (Nottingham: Shoestring Press, 2006), copyright Christopher Southgate. I am grateful to Chris Southgate and Shoestring Press for permission to reproduce these lines. I also thank Chris for generously allowing me to quote from his unpublished lecture 'Poetry and Science', given at St Stephen's Church, Exeter, October 2018.

This book is dedicated to the memory of my former colleague, the Revd Professor D. P. Davies. When I began my university career at what was then the University of Wales, Lampeter, D. P. was a wonderfully supportive colleague, mentor and friend to me, as to many who worked with him over the years. His extraordinary knowledge of the world of theology and higher education made him a source of endless wise counsel – not to mention a rich fund of stories, particularly over a beer or two. His network of students, colleagues and associates was literally global, and a great many people around the world will remember him with immense respect, affection and gratitude. May he rest in peace and rise in glory.

Neil Messer,
Winchester, October 2019

1

Setting up the dialogue

CHAPTER SUMMARY

This book is based on a typology or classification of encounters between science and Christian theology. In this chapter I introduce the typology, which runs as follows. If we wish to understand ourselves and the world in relation to God, we can think of this as a conversation between two voices: a 'voice of the Christian tradition' and the voice of the relevant scientific discipline. In that case, what weight should be given to each voice in developing our understanding, and what kind of contribution should each voice make? Five types of answer can be imagined:

(1)   Only the scientific voice contributes, and the contribution of the Christian tradition is denied or dismissed.

(2)   Both voices contribute, but the scientific voice plays the predominant role in shaping the dialogue and addressing the questions. The claims of the Christian tradition must be adjusted where necessary to fit an account whose shape and content are determined by science.

(3)   Both voices contribute, and neither predominates in shaping the dialogue or answering the questions.

(4)   Both voices contribute, but the voice of the Christian tradition plays the predominant role in shaping the encounter and addressing the questions.

(5) Only the voice of the Christian tradition contributes, and the contribution of the scientific voice is denied or dismissed.

In later chapters, this typology will be tested out by analysing in detail three examples of important topics in the science and theology field: how to understand divine action in the light of contemporary physics, evolution and the problem of 'natural evil', and the significance of scientific studies of religion. This introductory chapter closes with some suggestions for how different kinds of readers might use the book.

1.1 Introduction

When theology and science encounter one another, how should this be done? That is broadly what this book is about. It has three main aims: (1) to set out a typology (or classification) of ways in which science–theology encounters might be set up, (2) to test the typology on three important debates in science and theology, and (3) to draw some conclusions about how science–theology encounters *should* be conducted. If I achieve these aims, I hope that will make the book interesting and useful to students and scholars designing research projects in science and theology. I hope it will also be of use to readers interested in the particular issues I shall use as examples, or in the field in general. At the end of this chapter, I make some more detailed suggestions about how these various kinds of readers might use the book.

Before introducing the typology, I need to define some terms and do a little groundwork.

1.2 'Science and religion' or 'science and theology'?

Sometimes this field is referred to as 'science and religion', at other times 'science and theology'. The subject matter and the people involved are largely the same in either case, yet some scholars definitely prefer one term or the other.[1] What do the different terms suggest?

The word 'religion' often names a human phenomenon that can be scientifically investigated (see Chapter 4). It is also used for particular faith traditions: Christianity, Judaism, Hinduism and so on are referred to as 'religions'. Both uses have their problems. Indeed, within the field of religious studies, there is lively debate about what 'religion' might mean, and whether it is even a helpful category for academic study.[2] 'Theology' literally means 'God-talk'. More precisely, it describes some kind of intellectually rigorous, critical articulation and exploration of a faith tradition and its implications. It is most often used to describe this kind of thinking about Christian faith, though it is also used of some other religious traditions. As Philip Hefner points out, it is an *in*appropriate term for some faiths.[3] Yet many of the topics identified as 'religion and science' issues[4] would naturally be seen as *theological*, by Christians at least.

We should also keep in mind that the uses of both terms, 'religion' and 'theology', have changed greatly over time, so what we understand by them now may not be what was meant in earlier eras.[5] 'Science' is another term whose meanings and uses have shifted over time,[6] and it, too, is surprisingly tricky to define. The disciplines labelled sciences (in English) are diverse in their subject matter and methods. It is far from easy to say what they have in common, if anything, that identifies them as sciences. Those discussed in this book all rely in some way on gathering data about the natural world through observation and experiment, and constructing theories to account for the data and/or make testable

---

[1]Compare (for example) Michael Welker, 'Science and Theology: Their Relation at the Beginning of the Third Millenium [*sic*]', and Philip Hefner, 'Religion-and-Science', in Philip Clayton (ed.), *The Oxford Handbook of Religion and Science* (Oxford: Oxford University Press, 2008), pp. 551–61 and 562–76, respectively.

[2]See Maya Warrier and Simon Oliver (eds), *Theology and Religious Studies: An Exploration of Disciplinary Boundaries* (London: T & T Clark, 2008).

[3]Hefner, 'Religion-and-Science', p. 569.

[4]For example, in Clayton, *The Oxford Handbook of Religion and Science*.

[5]See Peter Harrison, *The Territories of Science and Religion* (Chicago: University of Chicago Press, 2015), pp. 7–11, 16–18.

[6]Ibid., pp. 11–16.

predictions. However, the forms these activities take and the ways they relate to one another vary greatly from one science to another.

This book is about how science, understood in this way, interacts with Christian theology. One of my reasons for giving the book this focus is that I am a Christian theologian, so this is the tradition I am best qualified to write about. It was also where the contemporary field of science and theology/religion was mostly focused in its early days, though more recently there has been a welcome growth in the literature on science and other religious traditions.[7] While this book focuses on *Christian* theology, I hope it will be interesting and useful to those working in, or on, other faiths – even if my specific arguments and proposals may not be directly transferable.

1.3 Kinds of questions in science and theology

We can ask various kinds of questions about the interaction of science and theology. Some are *historical*. For example: How have interactions between (what we call) science and theology changed over time? What is the history of particular debates and disputes? Others are *methodological*: How should we investigate issues in science and theology? Then there are *substantive* questions about particular topics in science and theology. For example: How should we think of God's action in the world in light of contemporary physics (see Chapter 2)? What are the implications of evolutionary biology for Christian faith in an all-powerful, perfectly good Creator (Chapter 3)? Many interactions of science with theology also raise questions about *ethics*: the right, the good and how we ought to live and act in the world. These can operate at various levels: metaethics (including questions about the nature and meaning of moral concepts), normative ethics (how to make moral decisions) and practical ethics (how we should behave).

There is not much discussion of ethics in this book, though I have written extensively elsewhere about questions in ethics that arise from the interactions of science and theology.[8] The present

---

[7]See Clayton, *The Oxford Handbook of Religion and Science*, chs. 1–7.
[8]See, for example, Neil Messer, *Selfish Genes and Christian Ethics: Theological and Ethical Reflections on Evolutionary Biology* (London: SCM, 2007) and *Theological*

book is mostly about methodology: how to set up encounters between science and theology. This has some dangers. Michael Welker warns that prolonged discussions of methodology can become 'stale and unproductive'.[9] Or, as Jeffrey Stout once put it, 'Preoccupation with method is like clearing your throat: it can go on for only so long before you lose your audience.'[10] Furthermore, accounts of methodology can be counterproductive, distorting the investigations they are supposed to clarify and assist. As we shall see in the next section, a number of critics believe that methodological talk in science and theology has done just this. For this reason, John Perry and Sarah Lane Ritchie have gone so far as to propose a 'moratorium' on methodology in this field.[11]

I am sympathetic to these criticisms. However, as Welker emphasizes, in this interdisciplinary field, we cannot avoid methodological questions.[12] In the next two sections I shall explain how my methodological proposal avoids the dangers highlighted by critics like Perry and Ritchie. As for Stout's warning about losing one's audience, to try and stop this book becoming too abstract and tedious, I link my methodological discussion to three important substantive topics. These focus on contemporary rather than historical debates, though in the next section I shall draw on critical historical perspectives to inform the way the discussion is set up.

1.4 Classifications, typologies and the problems of talking about 'science and theology'

This book is based on a typology, or classification, of ways in which theology may interact with science. There have been numerous

---

Neuroethics: Christian Ethics Meets the Science of the Human Brain (London: Bloomsbury T & T Clark, 2017).

[9]Welker, 'Science and Theology', p. 553.

[10]Jeffrey Stout, *Ethics after Babel: The Languages of Morals and Their Discontents* (Boston: Beacon Press, 1988), p. 163.

[11]John Perry and Sarah Lane Ritchie, 'Magnets, Magic, and Other Anomalies: In Defense of Methodological Naturalism', *Zygon* 53, no. 4 (2018), pp. 1064–93 (p. 1089).

[12]Welker, 'Science and Theology', p. 553.

typologies of science and theology/religion before mine. The best known and most widely used was devised by Ian Barbour, who described four views of the relationship between science and religion: conflict, independence, dialogue and integration.[13] Since Barbour produced his typology, a number of other leading scholars have proposed modifications and refinements of it and alternatives to it (see Box 1.1).

BOX 1.1: TYPOLOGIES IN SCIENCE AND THEOLOGY/RELIGION

Several authors in the science and theology field have proposed typologies intended to modify, refine, complement or replace Barbour's. Some of the leading examples are as follows:

- *Philip Clayton's* book *God and Contemporary Science* lists 'the *sorts of ways*' in which different authors claim 'scientific cosmology can contribute to theological conclusions … [and] scientific work stands in need of an interpretive framework of the sort that theology … offers'.[14] These can be arranged along a continuum: (1) 'science leads to theology'; (2) 'science … supports one particular religious viewpoint'; (3) 'science by itself amounts to a sort of religious perspective'; (4) science supports *multiple* religious perspectives'; (5) some authors 'find spirituality in or implied by science … while resisting making any truth claims on this basis'; (6) 'science and theology [are] two distinct activities which have nothing to do with each other'; (7) 'theology is a pure construct, and naturalism represents the best truth we have about the world'.[15]
- In the late 1990s, *Niels Henrik Gregersen* and *J. Wentzel van Huyssteen* assembled a volume in which six authors

---

[13]Barbour's typology can be found in several of his works, including Ian G. Barbour, *When Science Meets Religion* (San Francisco, CA: HarperSanFrancisco, 2000).
[14]Philip D. Clayton, *God and Contemporary Science* (Edinburgh: Edinburgh University Press, 1997), p. 127, emphasis original.
[15]Ibid., pp. 155–6, emphasis in original.

proposed different models for 'rethinking' the theology–
science dialogue: postfoundationalism 'beyond conflict
and consonance', critical realism, naturalism, pragmatism,
'science and theology as complementary perspectives' and
finally, a 'contextual coherence theory'.[16]

- Around the same time, *Ted Peters* produced an eightfold
  scheme expanding on Barbour's typology, with categories
  ranging from 'scientism' through 'hypothetical consonance'
  to 'ethical overlap' and 'New Age spirituality'.[17]

- *John Polkinghorne*, writing in the mid-2000s, suggested that
  a more fine-grained typology than Barbour's was needed,
  describing the 'kinds of positive interaction that have
  actually been taking place',[18] and classifying not just the
  methods but the content of the interactions. The four kinds
  of interactions he identified, he labelled 'deistic', 'theistic',
  'revisionary' and 'developmental'.[19] He suggested that there
  was an unmet need for a fifth type, led by theologians rather
  than scientists, which could be called 'systematic'.[20]

- *Mikael Stenmark* has more recently set out a scheme
  of four models, which he calls 'irreconcilability',
  'reconciliation', 'independence' and 'replacement'.[21]
  However, he thinks some of these models need to be
  subdivided and nuanced in various ways; for example,
  he identifies 'conservative', 'traditional', 'liberal' and
  (postmodern) 'constructivist' versions of the reconciliation
  model.[22]

---

[16]Niels Henrik Gregersen and J. Wentzel van Huyssteen (eds), *Rethinking Theology and Science: Six Models for the Current Dialogue* (Grand Rapids, MI: Eerdmans, 1998).

[17]Ted Peters, 'Theology and the Natural Sciences', in David F. Ford (ed.), *The Modern Theologians*, 2nd ed. (Oxford: Blackwell, 1997), pp. 649–67 (pp. 650–4).

[18]John Polkinghorne, *Science and the Trinity: The Christian Encounter with Reality* (London: SPCK, 2004), p. 11.

[19]Ibid., pp. 11–29.

[20]Ibid., pp. 31–2.

[21]Mikael Stenmark, 'Ways of Relating Science and Religion', in Peter Harrison (ed.), *The Cambridge Companion to Science and Religion* (Cambridge: Cambridge University Press, 2010), pp. 278–95 (pp. 278–80).

[22]Ibid., pp. 287–90.

However, typologies in general and Barbour's in particular have received a good deal of criticism. For example, Geoffrey Cantor and Chris Kenny have argued that Barbour's typology is unhelpful in understanding the relationships of science and religion, particularly historically.[23] One of their criticisms is that it lends undue weight to the so-called conflict thesis, the claim that science and religion are inevitably in conflict and always have been. Cantor and Kenny complain that Barbour's typology unwittingly supports the conflict thesis, because it takes conflict as the starting point and presents the other types as alternatives to conflict. Conflict thus becomes the default position for science–religion relationships, even though that was not Barbour's intention.

Another of Cantor and Kenny's criticisms, which could apply to many typologies, is that they treat 'science' and 'religion' as **essentialist** categories or **reified** entities. In other words, they present a picture of a thing called 'science', with a fixed, stable meaning and clearly defined boundaries, which exists in some kind of relationship to another stable and clearly defined thing called 'religion'. According to Cantor and Kenny, this misrepresents a more complex and untidy historical and contemporary reality. This can lead to serious misunderstandings of historical events, such as the conflict between Galileo and the hierarchy of the Catholic Church.

The historian Peter Harrison has developed similar concerns into a critique of the whole way of describing and thinking of this field as 'science and religion'.[24] He argues that it is a remarkably recent development in Western culture to think of science and religion as distinct entities, which could be in a relationship such as conflict or dialogue with each other. This has involved some major shifts from earlier understandings of 'science' and 'religion' (or the Latin terms from which they were derived).

According to Harrison, in the middle ages the Latin terms *scientia* and *religio* both referred primarily to virtues or inner dispositions.

---

[23]Geoffrey Cantor and Chris Kenny, 'Barbour's Fourfold Way: Problems with His Taxonomy of Science-Religion Relationships', *Zygon* 36, no. 4 (2001), pp. 765–81. For a response, see Ian G. Barbour, 'On Typologies for Relating Science and Religion', *Zygon* 37, no. 2 (2002), pp. 345–59.
[24]Harrison, *The Territories of Science and Religion.*

Scientia was a mental habit that made one skilled at deriving truths from first principles, while *religio* was a disposition to do with prayer and piety.[25] It was in the early modern age that the familiar uses of 'religion' and 'religions', which I described earlier, first arose.[26] The way we use the word 'science' has even more recent origins. It began in the nineteenth century, as a way to refer to the increasingly professionalized activities that had previously been called 'natural philosophy' and 'natural history'. To establish the professional status of this newly defined activity of 'science', it was necessary to mark out its boundaries and say what it was *not*: in particular, to exclude religion.[27] Like other historians, Harrison therefore sees the conflict thesis as (in effect) a late nineteenth-century tactic for asserting the status of the new scientific profession.[28] Echoing Cantor and Kenny, he warns that those who argue for a more positive relationship continue to use the categories in the same way. Ironically, this 'has the potential to reinforce the very conditions that make conflict possible. Advocates of constructive dialogue are thus unknowingly complicit in the perpetuation of conflict.'[29]

In similar vein, the physicist Tom McLeish objects to the framing of the science–theology relationship as 'science *and* theology'. He argues that the connections between what we call 'science' and 'theology' are much closer, and go back much further in human history, than we usually imagine. It therefore distorts the picture to think of them as two separate domains whose relationship – whether separation, conflict or constructive dialogue – is best described by the word 'and'. Instead, he argues, what is needed is a 'theology *of* science', as well as a 'science of theology'.[30]

---

[25]Ibid., pp. 7–8, 12–14, 55–81. According to Harrison, the meaning of 'theology' has also shifted over time, only acquiring something like its present use from the late middle ages onwards: ibid., pp. 17–18.

[26]Ibid., pp. 83–116.

[27]Ibid., pp. 145–82.

[28]Major culprits included Thomas Henry Huxley and his friends in England, and John William Draper and Andrew Dickson White in America: see ibid., pp. 162–4, 171–5. As Harrison observes, some of the 'historical' examples of science–religion conflict described by Draper and White were complete falsehoods.

[29]Ibid., p. 198.

[30]Tom McLeish, *Faith and Wisdom in Science* (Oxford: Oxford University Press, 2014), pp. 166–72 (emphasis added).

A related concern is voiced by Perry and Ritchie, who are highly critical of the kind of methodological discussion represented by the typologies in Box 1.1.[31] Part of their concern is that the categories of 'science' and 'religion' are overly broad, so to ask in this broadbrush way how 'science' should relate to 'religion' is unlikely to be helpful or informative. They recommend instead focusing on *particular* disciplines, topics and questions, and working out ad hoc the methodologies needed to address them.[32]

In short, familiar ways of thinking about the relationships between what we call 'science', 'religion' and 'theology' (such as the typologies surveyed earlier) may lead to serious distortions and damaging misunderstandings. Yet as Harrison acknowledges, the familiar categories of 'science' and 'religion' are firmly entrenched in contemporary culture and unlikely to change radically any time soon. Moreover, the scientific study of nature and human nature will continue to generate findings with all kinds of implications for religious belief, thought and practice. So, is it possible to think of encounters between theology and science in a way that avoids the distortions criticized by Harrison and McLeish?

Like McLeish, I am unhappy with the 'and' in 'science *and* theology'. However, I propose a different change, to 'science *in* theology'. In other words, the key question I think we should be asking is this: What part do the findings, theories and perspectives that we call 'scientific' play – and what part *should* they play – in shaping our understanding of ourselves, other living things and the cosmos in relation to God; the kind of understanding we call 'theological'? Taking up Perry and Ritchie's concern about overbroad categories, we should ask this question not in relation to 'science' and 'theology' in general, but about *particular* issues, scientific disciplines and areas of theological enquiry. The next section will further develop this way of framing the discussion.

---

[31]Perry and Ritchie, 'Magnets, Magic, and Other Anomalies', pp. 1084–9.
[32]Their example of an unhelpfully broad question is, 'What do science and religion say about ... evolution?', whereas 'What can neuroscience of addictions and the Eastern Orthodox liturgy teach us about moral habit formation?' is an example of a better question: ibid., p. 1086.

1.5 Science *in* theology: Five types and three examples

If we wish to understand ourselves and the world in relation to God, what contribution to that understanding should we expect from scientific disciplines, and how should that contribution relate to other sources of theological understanding, particularly the Bible?

Asking the question in this way shows it to be a special case of a familiar question about the sources of Christian theology. These are often summarized as:

- *Scripture*: the books of the Hebrew Bible (Old Testament) and New Testament, which most Christian communities regard as having a special and distinctive authority for their faith and practice. However, there are widely varying views about the nature of that authority.[33] Indeed, even what counts as 'scripture' is contested to some extent: Protestant, Catholic and Orthodox churches have different 'canons', or collections of books recognized as Scripture, though these have a great deal in common.

- *Tradition*: this may simply mean something like 'the Church's time-honored practices of worship, service and critical reflection'.[34] However, it sometimes denotes more than just this, as in official Catholic teaching: 'Tradition [with a capital 'T'] transmits in its entirety the Word of God which has been entrusted to the apostles by Christ the Lord and the Holy Spirit.'[35]

- *Reason*: This is a complex heading – by definition, any kind of theological *thinking* involves the use of reason, in interpreting biblical texts or church teaching, in arguing for particular conclusions and so on. But 'reason' is sometimes viewed as a distinct source of theology, in the sense that

---

[33]For a collection of essays illustrating this variety, see Angus Paddison (ed.), *Theologians on Scripture* (London: Bloomsbury T & T Clark, 2016).

[34]Richard B. Hays, *The Moral Vision of the New Testament: Community, Cross, New Creation* (San Francisco, CA: HarperSanFrancisco, 1996), p. 210.

[35]*Catechism of the Catholic Church*, para. 81, online at http://www.vatican.va/arc hive/ENG0015/_INDEX.HTM (accessed 24 September 2019).

humans might be able to learn something about God and God's ways with the world by using their own reason, quite apart from what God might have revealed through scripture or tradition.

- *Experience*: This could include 'religious' or 'spiritual' experience, as well as human experience more generally.

If the sources of theology are understood in this way, theologians need to decide how much weight they should give to each source, and what *kind* of contribution each can make to theological understanding.

Considering the science–theology relationship specifically, science is often regarded in our time as the paradigm of reason. Indeed, some scientific secularists seem to think science is the *only* valid form of reason: the complete opposite of 'faith', which is supposed to be irrational and even anti-rational.[36] Needless to say, any serious theologian would vigorously dispute this. In any event, the sciences represent particular forms of rational enquiry, but it is worth noting that almost any science also relies on structured and controlled kinds of *experience*, in the form of experiments, observations and suchlike ways of collecting data. So the question about the contribution of science to theological understanding is really a way of asking how the particular combinations of reason and experience that we call 'sciences' relate to scripture and tradition (as well as other forms of reason and experience) in shaping theological understanding.

To simplify this a little, imagine a conversation between two voices about some aspect of nature or human nature in relation to God. One we might call *a voice of the Christian tradition*. By this I mean a voice that combines scripture and tradition in some way.[37] It has its origins in the scriptures, and it has been shaped by the Christian churches' history of reflection and practice down

---

[36]For a particularly trenchant expression of this view, see Peter Atkins, 'Science and Atheism', in Clayton, *The Oxford Handbook of Religion and Science*, pp. 124–36.

[37]It is difficult to avoid the awkwardness and clumsiness of using the word 'tradition' in (at least) two different senses here. I hope this paragraph makes clear enough the distinction between 'the Christian tradition' – the historical and contemporary understanding and practice of Christian faith by the Christian church in all its diversity – and 'tradition' in the sense of a source of Christian theology, as defined at the beginning of this section.

the centuries. This voice will be imagined differently in different branches of Christianity. For many Protestants, scripture is the divinely inspired supreme authority for Christian faith and life, and the role of tradition is the subservient one of helping us interpret scripture rightly. In official Catholic teaching, scripture and tradition are 'distinct modes of transmission' of God's word, which together contain the '"Sacred deposit" of the faith'.[38] Some Orthodox theologians speak of 'Holy Tradition',[39] an integrated whole which begins with the scriptures but also includes the faith and life of the church, particularly the Fathers (the theologians of the early church) and the councils which brought together leaders from the whole church.

It is also important to note that feminist, liberationist and other contextual theologies raise critical questions about the way power operates in the Christian tradition. Who has had most influence on how this tradition is understood, and who has been sidelined or silenced? When I refer to 'the Christian tradition', I do not mean to suggest a uniform whole that speaks with a single universally agreed voice. Borrowing Alasdair MacIntyre's words, what I mean is something more like 'an historically extended, socially embodied argument',[40] including an ongoing argument about what the Christian tradition actually *is*.

The other voice in the conversation is the voice of a scientific discipline. Of course, there may be a number of scientific voices from different disciplines that have a bearing on a particular issue or debate. But to keep it simple, think of the dialogue (for the time being) as a conversation between *a* scientific voice and a voice of the Christian tradition.

If we think of it in this way, the question becomes: *How much, and what, should each of these voices contribute to the theological understanding we are trying to develop?* In general terms, we can imagine five possible answers:[41]

---

[38]*Catechism of the Catholic Church*, paras 80, 84.

[39]For example, John Breck, *Scripture in Tradition: The Bible and Its Interpretation in the Orthodox Church* (Crestwood, NY: St Vladimir's Seminary Press, 2001).

[40]Alasdair MacIntyre, *After Virtue: A Study in Moral Theory*, 2nd ed. (London: Duckworth, 1985), p. 222.

[41]I originally developed this typology some years ago as a heuristic device to help structure a dialogue between evolutionary biology and theological ethics: Messer, *Selfish Genes*

(1) *Only the scientific voice contributes, and the contribution of the Christian tradition is denied or dismissed.*

Accounts of this type, in one way or another, reduce theological to scientific discourse or use science to displace scripture and tradition as sources of knowledge and understanding. Scientific accounts of nature might be considered superior to accounts grounded in scripture and tradition, because the former are evidence-based and intellectually rigorous while the latter are not.[42] Or it might be said that scientific accounts are objective and universally valid while those based in scripture and tradition are not.

This type of account often promotes some form of scientific materialism or atheism (though not always, as we shall see). It may therefore seem strange to describe this type as one in which only science contributes to a *theological* understanding of the world. Yet someone who asserts that science shows that 'God almost certainly does not exist'[43] is making a claim about God, albeit a negative one. So this type of science–theology encounter can be understood as a proposal about the proper sources of theological (or perhaps a-theological) understanding.

(2) *Both voices contribute, but the scientific voice plays the predominant role in shaping the dialogue and addressing the questions.*[44] *The claims of the Christian tradition must be adjusted*

---

and Christian Ethics, pp. 49–62. Since then I have used it (with changes and developments in its formulation) in other dialogues between theology and the biosciences, particularly but not only in relation to ethical questions: see Neil Messer, *Theological Neuroethics: Christian Ethics Meets the Science of the Human Brain* (London: Bloomsbury T & T Clark, 2017), pp. 24–37. Formulating it in terms of the 'voices' of the Christian tradition and a scientific discipline is a new development for this book, which is intended to clarify how the typology works and respond to the concerns of Harrison and McLeish, discussed earlier. The influence of Hans Frei, *Types of Christian Theology*, ed. George Hunsinger and William H. Placher (New Haven, CT: Yale University Press, 1992) on my typology will be evident, though mine was developed in a different context for a different purpose and is not simply equivalent to Frei's. For a relatively recent discussion of Frei's typology, see Paul J. DeHart, *The Trial of the Witnesses: The Rise and Decline of Postliberal Theology* (Oxford: Blackwell, 2006), ch. 5.

[42]For example, Atkins, 'Science and Atheism'.

[43]Richard Dawkins, *The God Delusion* (London: Black Swan, 2007), p. 189.

[44]'Predominant' is intended to suggest the weight or prominence given to one voice in the dialogue, rather than an exercise of power or domination by those representing

where necessary to fit an account whose shape and content are determined by science.

In the second type of encounter, the claims of the Christian tradition might be evaluated and justified according to the standards and criteria of natural science, and might have to be modified in response to scientific challenges. What differentiates this type from the next (type 3) is that in type 2, the direction of the critique is largely one way. Even core Christian beliefs and theological affirmations may be criticized and reshaped quite radically in light of a scientific view of the world. By comparison, that scientific view is regarded much more confidently, and type 2 authors will be less inclined to critique or reshape it in light of Scripture and Christian tradition.

For some influential authors, the choice of this type has a strongly 'apologetic' motivation. They aim to defend Christian belief against scientific challenges, or they appeal to scientific evidence and arguments to demonstrate the credibility of the Christian faith.[45] For some (as we shall see in later chapters), the choice to work in a type 2 way is deliberate and explicit, while others seem to drift into it without intending to.

(3) Both voices contribute, and neither predominates in shaping the dialogue or answering the questions.

In type 3, the voices of science and the Christian tradition both contribute to the account, but neither voice dominates. As in type 2, Christian beliefs and theological claims may be questioned and

---

one or other voice.

[45]One example is Arthur Peacocke, who believed that the credibility of the Christian faith could only be restored if Christian beliefs were reshaped to conform more closely to a scientific view of the world: see 'Science and the Future of Theology: Critical Issues', *Zygon* 35, no. 1 (2000), pp. 119–40. It may seem surprising to describe this as an 'apologetic' stance, since apologetics is sometimes thought of as the defence of a fairly fixed understanding of Christian faith, whereas Peacocke wanted to *revise* the understanding of the Christian faith quite radically. However, if apologetics is understood more generally as making a rational case for Christian belief and defending it against sceptical challenges, that was certainly one of Peacocke's aims. As in Peacocke's case, when the credibility of Christian belief is seen to rely heavily on science-based arguments, there will be a strong motivation to revise or jettison Christian claims that seem to be in tension with scientific findings or perspectives.

criticized on the basis of scientific knowledge and theory. However, a type 3 encounter offers more scope for challenge and critique to operate also in the other direction: for a scientifically formed view of the world to be critiqued, reshaped or extended in light of the Christian tradition.

As with type 2, there is sometimes an apologetic element in type 3 accounts, but this tends to be less prominent and less dependent on science. Authors working in this way are more likely to say that their reasons for Christian belief do not depend on scientific evidence or arguments. Some, echoing the mediaeval theologian Anselm of Canterbury, will describe their work as 'faith seeking understanding'.[46] Many science and theology scholars aim to work in a type 3 way, though, as we shall see in later chapters, they do not always do so consistently.

(4) *Both voices contribute, but the voice of the Christian tradition plays the predominant role in shaping the encounter and addressing the questions.*

The fourth type of encounter between science and the Christian tradition operates, to borrow Karl Barth's terminology, in 'dogmatic' rather than 'apologetic' mode.[47] Those working in this way are not trying to demonstrate the credibility of Christian belief in the face of modern science or to defend Christian faith from scientific challenges. Their confidence in the Christian faith does not depend on being able to demonstrate that science supports it.

Depending on the particular branch of Christianity within which this kind of account is located, its understanding of the Christian faith might (for example) be shaped first and foremost by the scriptures, or by scripture and church tradition interacting in a more equal way, or by 'Holy Tradition' understood in the

---

[46]See Thomas Williams, 'Saint Anselm', in Edward N. Zalta (ed.), *The Stanford Encyclopedia of Philosophy* (Spring 2016 Edition), section 2.1. Online at https ://plato.stanford.edu/archives/spr2016/entries/anselm/ (accessed 28 November 2018). One example is Robert John Russell, 'Quantum Theory and the Theology of Non-interventionist Objective Divine Action', in Philip Clayton (ed.), *The Oxford Handbook of Religion and Science* (Oxford: Oxford University Press, 2008), pp. 579–95 (p. 584).
[47]See Karl Barth, *Church Dogmatics*, ed. G. W Bromiley and T. F. Torrance, 13 vols (Edinburgh: T & T Clark, 1956–75), vol. 2.2, § 36.1.

Orthodox way described earlier. Whichever is the case, authors of such accounts will be willing to appropriate scientific perspectives and insights critically into a theological understanding shaped by those time-honoured sources of Christian faith. In type 4, theology can be highly hospitable to insights and questions from the natural sciences, and scientific questions and challenges may prompt some rethinking of *how* Scripture and tradition should be understood and interpreted. However, the voice of the Christian tradition remains the predominant one in shaping theological understanding.

Until recently, this approach has been rare in the science and theology literature, and it has often been regarded rather unfavourably. However, in recent years, growing numbers of science and theology scholars have worked in something like this way, and we shall explore various examples in later chapters.

(5) *Only the voice of the Christian tradition contributes, and the contribution of the scientific voice is denied or dismissed.*
The fifth type is almost a mirror image of the first: of our two voices, only the Christian tradition is thought to have anything to say. This might take the form of denying the scientific voice's validity, as when young-earth creationists deny evolutionary biology. Alternatively, the scientific voice may be seen as valid in its own sphere but thought to have nothing to say about questions of faith or theology, as in Stephen Jay Gould's proposal that science and religion should be considered as 'non-overlapping magisteria' or 'NOMA'.[48] Gould advocated 'a respectful, even loving, concordat between the magisteria of science and religion',[49] in which each must respect the boundary between their two territories, and neither science nor religion should trespass into the other's domain.

This description of the five types may seem rather abstract and schematic. To try and make it more concrete and specific, in Chapters 2–4 I use the typology to analyse three important areas of debate in the science and theology literature. These are the following:

---

[48]Stephen Jay Gould, *Rocks of Ages: Science and Religion in the Fulness of Life* (London: Vintage, 2002).
[49]Ibid., p. 9.

- Divine action (Chapter 2): How (if at all) can Christian theology think of God acting in the world, in the light of the contemporary physical sciences?
- Evolution, natural evil and **theodicy** (Chapter 3): How (if at all) can Christians speak of God's goodness and power in the face of the suffering, death and destruction inherent in the process of biological evolution?
- The evolution, cognitive science and neuroscience of religion (Chapter 4): What implications do these approaches to the scientific study of religion have for Christian theology?

In each of these chapters, the typology is used to classify different accounts from a selection of influential authors. This tests its usefulness as a scheme for organizing these sometimes highly complex debates and helping us understand what is going on in them. It also enables us to evaluate the different types of account, and to assess the strengths and weaknesses of each. These chapters therefore test both the 'descriptive' and 'normative' value of the typology: how well it describes the ways in which science and the Christian tradition actually *do* interact, and the light it sheds on how they *ought to* interact. I hope my analyses of the three topics will also make an interesting contribution to the discussion of the issues themselves. I should emphasize, though, that my coverage of the issues is not comprehensive, since each is a major science–theology topic with an extensive literature. On each topic, I do not attempt to survey all the relevant literature or all the major authors, but simply choose representative examples of the main positions.

Chapter 5 draws together the conclusions from Chapters 2–4, offering some proposals for how to use the typology and how encounters of theology with science should be set up. This chapter also addresses one aspect not considered so far. For simplicity's sake, the typology only considers the contributions of two voices: those of science and the Christian tradition. But in almost any of these dialogues, there will be other voices with their own contributions to make. Chapter 5 discusses the contributions that might come from philosophical voices, and from creative and artistic voices.[50]

---

[50]My discussion of Harrison in section 1.4 suggests that it is over-simple to think of these as separate voices distinct from the voice(s) of the Christian tradition. The

1.6 Possible difficulties and objections

At this point it may be helpful to deal with a few potential difficulties. First, although I have criticized the language of 'science *and* theology', it will not always be possible to avoid that language. We are where we are, and much of the existing literature frames the relationship as 'and'. However, I shall try to keep the focus as clearly as possible on the question about 'science *in* theology': the part science plays and should play in shaping theological understanding.

Second, my proposal is still limited in some ways. In particular, it still focuses more on the cognitive aspects of faith (theological *understanding*) than on practices of prayer, worship and discipleship. But historically, these practices have been (if anything) the more important aspects and purposes of theological work. This is a real limitation of my typology, but the cognitive questions are nonetheless important ones to ask as part of the whole picture of Christian faith and life. Moreover, framing the issue as 'science *in* theology' perhaps more clearly signals the possibility that theological reflection on scientific views of the world could shape Christian worship and practice, as well as Christian thinking. We shall see hints, at least, of some of these connections in later chapters.

Third, my approach might seem insufficiently ambitious, since it treats the framing of science–theology encounters mostly as an issue for *theology*: How should theological understandings be shaped by scientific insights? By contrast, for example, Robert John Russell's approach of 'Creative Mutual Interaction' (CMI) between science and theology envisages a series of ways in which science could influence theology, but also some ways *theology* could influence *science*.[51] However, the approach I am proposing actually makes quite a radical claim about the relationship of science to theology. Science and theology are not to be thought of as distinct domains

---

relationship is more complex than that: for much of Christian history, 'voices of the Christian tradition' have been in part philosophical voices, and (in a different way) in part artistic voices. Yet at other times, these voices have defined themselves over against the Christian tradition. The discussion in Chapter 5 brings out something of this complexity.

[51]See Robert John Russell and Kirk Wegter-McNelly, 'Science and Theology: Mutual Interaction', in Ted Peters and Gaymon Bennett (eds), *Bridging Science and Religion* (London: SCM Press, 2002), pp. 19–34 (esp. pp. 33–4).

of enquiry, like territories on a map, which might be separate, overlapping, merged or whose border might be a conflict zone. Instead, theology is concerned with the biggest picture possible: its subject matter, in principle, is *everything* in relation to God. In that light, the question about 'science *in* theology' asks what contribution scientific views of particular aspects of reality might make to that big picture. Moreover, as I have explained, my approach imagines the science–theology encounter as a dialogue involving two or more voices. It is entirely possible, at least in principle, that scientific partners in such dialogues might come away from the conversation with their understanding and practice changed in some respects, perhaps including some of those envisaged by Russell.

1.7 To various kinds of readers: Ways you could use this book

At the beginning of this chapter, I stated three aims for the book: (1) to set out a typology of ways in which science–theology encounters might be set up, (2) to test the typology on three important debates in science and theology and (3) to draw some conclusions about how science–theology encounters should be conducted. The first of these has been done in the previous sections. Chapters 2–4 are concerned with the second aim, and the third will be addressed in Chapter 5.

The book has been written with various kinds of readers in mind, who might wish to use it in different ways. The most obvious, of course, is to read it from beginning to end. Those who are interested in critically examining the whole argument in sequence – how I use the typology to analyse particular issues, the specific conclusions I draw about those issues and the general conclusions about encounters of science with theology that I draw from these case studies – will presumably use it in this way.

Others, though, might be mainly interested in using the typology for their own study, scholarship and research in the science–theology field. To aid this kind of use, I have included a chapter summary at the beginning of each chapter, and have made the summaries of Chapters 2–4 quite detailed. Those who are mostly interested in the typology and how to use it may choose to read the summaries of Chapters 2–4, and then the full text of the conclusions and proposals in Chapter 5. Anyone who then wishes to explore in more detail how those conclusions and proposals are supported by the test cases could refer back to any parts of Chapters 2–4 that are of particular interest.

Still others might be particularly interested in one or more of the topics discussed in Chapters 2–4, and the way I analyse the debates on those topics. Those who are mainly interested in these topics could choose to focus on one or more of Chapters 2–4. Since Chapter 5 explores how the treatment of these particular debates leads to more general conclusions about the relationship of science to Christian theology, such readers could refer to Chapter 5 if this more general question is of interest.

The science and theology literature is littered with technical terms from both theology and the natural sciences. It is also beset by initials and acronyms. To assist readers who may be unfamiliar with some of the terminology, I have included a Glossary and List of Abbreviations at the end of the book. Terms defined in the Glossary are set in bold the first time they are used. In Chapters 2–4 I have also used text boxes to explain some key concepts, theories and debates.

2

Divine action and contemporary science

CHAPTER SUMMARY

The first test case for my typology is the discussion of God's action in the world in the light of contemporary physics. Classical physics since Newton has suggested a deterministic, mechanistic account of the physical world, in which God's action is not needed to account for the way things are. Yet some twentieth-century developments, notably quantum mechanics and chaos theory, are said to raise questions about this deterministic picture. Do they make any difference to the way we should think about divine action?

The chapter begins by defining some key concepts and distinctions, including various kinds of *divine action*, different understandings of *the laws of nature*, *determinism* and various kinds of *causation* (see Boxes 2.2 and 2.3). I then identify and evaluate various accounts and proposals corresponding to the five types of approach described in Chapter 1 (see Chapter 1, 'Chapter Summary'). First, I discuss examples of the two extremes:

Type 1: Victor Stenger's view: the claim that there is a God who acts in the world can be tested scientifically, and science shows that it is false.

Type 5: Stephen Jay Gould's proposal that science and religion are 'non-overlapping magisteria' (NOMA), each valid in its own sphere but with no authority to enter the other's territory.

Either of these would rule out any dialogue about divine action between the voices of science and the Christian tradition, but I argue that both have serious enough flaws that they can be set aside.

I then consider examples of the three middle positions, which do allow for dialogues of different kinds:

Type 2: The Divine Action Project (DAP), a large and long-running collaborative project intended to develop 'scientific perspectives on divine action'. This often meant trying to identify **causal joints,** or aspects of the natural world through which an immaterial God could interact with material reality. The DAP had many participants who adopted diverse approaches, but the majority approach tended to give science a good deal of power to determine whether and how God can be said to act in the world.

Type 4: The 'theological turn'. This term is used by Sarah Lane Ritchie to describe various recent authors who give higher priority to theological perspectives in developing accounts of divine action. They challenge or question some important aspects of the DAP. Though Ritchie's description of the theological turn suggests my type 4, I argue that at least some theological-turn accounts are closer to type 3.

Type 3: I suggest that the work of some DAP participants and at least some theological-turn authors corresponds to this type. Ritchie herself, who is critical of both the DAP and the theological turn, calls for a kind of account that also seems to fit type 3.

The chapter concludes that type 2 (as represented by large parts of the DAP) places unwelcome restrictions on a Christian vision of how God acts in the world. Types 3 and 4 both allow for a rich theological engagement with scientific voices, but each is in danger of drifting towards one of the more problematic types. Each may be well placed to offer a check and correction to the dangers of the other. I conclude that in its first test, the typology proves helpful in analysing and understanding the extensive and complex debates about divine action and modern science.

2.1 Introduction

In the light of modern science, can we still say that God acts in the world, and if so, how? This question has probably done more than any other to define the science and theology field since the mid-twentieth century. It is raised by various scientific disciplines, but most obviously by the growth and development of physics since the days of Isaac Newton (1642–1727).

Newton himself was no mechanist, unlike some of his contemporaries. He and his followers believed God acts in the world in various ways: not only creating and sustaining the universe but (for example) controlling matter through active forces like gravitation, adjusting planetary motions from time to time, using natural phenomena like comets and plagues to intervene in human affairs and performing miracles.[1] Yet Newton's physics lent itself to a mechanistic and deterministic view of the universe (see Box 2.3) as a kind of clockwork system in which all physical states of affairs can be explained by physical causes alone. If the universe was like this, complete knowledge of its present state and physical laws would make it possible to predict its future precisely; as the French mathematician Laplace wrote in 1814, for 'an intelligence which could comprehend all the forces by which nature is animated and the respective situations of the beings who compose it … nothing would be uncertain and the future, as the past, would be present to its eyes'.[2]

If this is true, then as our understanding of these physical mechanisms grows, there will be less and less that requires God's action to explain it. For the seventeenth- and eighteenth-century **deists** God's role was restricted to the creation of the universe with the physical laws that govern its ongoing existence and events. Later it began to look more doubtful whether God was even needed to do that much. When Peter Atkins claimed in 1981 that an 'infinitely lazy creator' need not do anything at all to establish our

---

[1]Christopher Kaiser, *Creation and the History of Science* (London: Marshall Pickering, 1991), pp. 178–87, 191–5.
[2]Pierre Simon, Marquis de Laplace, *A Philosophical Essay on Probabilities*, trans. Frederick Wilson Truscott and Frederick Lincoln Emory (New York: John Wiley, 1902 (1814)), p. 4.

universe,[3] he was merely stating what had become received wisdom among scientific **materialists**.

In view of this, it became increasingly clear during the twentieth century that Christians were unwise to try and defend belief in God by looking for gaps in scientific explanations of the world and arguing that God was needed to fill those gaps. In 1944, the imprisoned German theologian Dietrich Bonhoeffer wrote to his friend Eberhard Bethge:

> We shouldn't think of God as the stopgap for the incompleteness of our knowledge, because then ... when the boundaries of knowledge are pushed ever further, God too is pushed further away and thus is ever on the retreat. We should find God in what we know, not in what we don't know; God wants to be grasped by us not in unsolved questions but in those that have been solved.[4]

These days, science and theology authors routinely reject a 'God of the gaps' view for exactly the reasons given by Bonhoeffer. However, in recent decades, many of these authors have also claimed that in a different sense, there *are* genuine gaps in the reality disclosed to us by science. These are not explanatory gaps of the kind that could be filled by doing more research, in the way Bonhoeffer recognized. There may be **ontological** gaps in the causal fabric of nature itself: in other words, it may be that not all natural events are fully determined by physical causes. There may also be **epistemological** gaps: limits to what *can* be known scientifically, even in principle.

Two twentieth-century developments in physics have particularly encouraged science and theology authors to make this claim. One is *quantum theory*. The laws of classical mechanics, such as Newton's laws of motion, allow the behaviour of everyday objects to be predicted very accurately. However, according to

---

[3]Peter Atkins, *The Creation* (London: W. H. Freeman, 1981), pp. 6–7.
[4]Dietrich Bonhoeffer, *Letters and Papers from Prison*, ed. Christian Gremmels, Eberhardt Bethge, Renate Bethge, Ilse Tödt and John W. de Gruchy and trans. Isabel Best, Lisa E. Dahill, Reinhard Krauss, Nancy Lukens, Barbara Rumscheidt, Martin Rumscheidt and Douglas W. Stott, Dietrich Bonhoeffer Works, 8 (Minneapolis, MN: Fortress, 2010), pp. 405–6.

quantum mechanics, the behaviour of very small objects like atoms or subatomic particles cannot be precisely predicted in this way. It can only be described or predicted statistically, in terms of probabilities. For example, if we have a large enough sample of a radioactive element, we can say quite precisely how long it will take for 50 per cent of the atomic nuclei in the sample to decay, but it is impossible to predict when any individual nucleus will decay. Moreover, measurement of a system will itself have an effect on that system. This is illustrated by the famous thought experiment of Schrödinger's cat (see Box 2.1).

Quantum mechanics gives a surprising and counter-intuitive picture of nature. It suggests that in all kinds of ways, the **microscopic** world at the scale of atoms or subatomic particles behaves very differently from our everyday experience of the **macroscopic** world. (Because the macroscopic world is made of atoms and subatomic particles, of course, the surprising results of quantum mechanics also raise questions about our everyday experience of the world.) Partly because this picture is so surprising, the mathematics and physics of quantum theory have been interpreted philosophically in various ways, some of which are listed in Box 2.1.

BOX 2.1: SCHRÖDINGER'S CAT AND INTERPRETATIONS OF QUANTUM MECHANICS

The physicist Erwin Schrödinger imagined a cat shut in a sealed box containing a single radioactive nucleus and a vial of poisonous gas. The nucleus has a 50 per cent chance of decaying over the duration of the experiment. If it does, the gas will be released from the vial and the cat will die. However, until we open the box, we have no way of knowing whether or not this has happened. All we can do is calculate the probabilities of the different states (e.g. the cat being alive or dead) at various times. These probabilities and the way they change over time can be described by a mathematical construct known as a *wave function*. The way the wave function of a system evolves over time is described mathematically by one of the most important equations of quantum mechanics, the Schrödinger equation. Opening the box is an example of a *measurement*, which in the context of quantum mechanics means an 'irreversible macroscopic registration of a state of affairs, and not simply conscious observation'.[5]

The mathematics of quantum mechanics fits experimental observations very well. But if we try to imagine in everyday terms the reality that it describes, we get a puzzling and paradoxical picture, as Schrödinger's cat illustrates. To try and make sense of these puzzles, the mathematics and physics of quantum theory have been interpreted philosophically in various ways, including the following:[6]

- *The Copenhagen (or orthodox) interpretation:* Until a system is measured, its various possible states exist simultaneously; they are 'superposed' on one another. The cat is both alive and dead. When a measurement takes place, the superposition is destroyed and the system collapses into one state: when the box is opened, the cat is either alive or dead. But the outcome is genuinely **indeterministic**: there is no physical cause that determines which of these states will exist after the measurement. (Schrödinger himself found this interpretation so unlikely that he devised his 'cat' thought experiment to show its absurdity. However, it remains the dominant interpretation.)

- *The hidden-variables interpretation:* Versions of this have been proposed by various authors, including David Bohm. Although the outcomes of quantum events *appear* random and undetermined to us, there are hidden causal factors determining their outcomes (such as a 'guiding wave' that determines the path taken by a moving particle). These hidden factors are unobservable *in principle*, not just because we do not have good enough measuring devices. So quantum events will always appear indeterministic to us, but in fact are fully deterministic.

---

[5]John Polkinghorne, *Faith, Science and Understanding* (London: SPCK, 2000), p. 120.

[6]For more detail on these and other interpretations, see Nicholas Saunders, *Divine Action and Modern Science* (Cambridge: Cambridge University Press, 2002), pp. 139–72.

- *The many-worlds interpretation*: There is a vast number of parallel worlds, and each possible state of a quantum system exists in one or more of these worlds; in an oft-quoted phrase, 'everything that can happen does happen'.[7] But these parallel worlds have no access to each other. So an observer in one world will open the box to find the cat alive, and will have no access to the parallel world in which the cat is dead.

The other development that questions a mechanistic view of the world is *chaos theory*. This is based on classical (Newtonian) mechanics, not quantum mechanics. In the twentieth century, physicists discovered that many systems are extremely sensitive to initial conditions. Imagine, for example, a frictionless pool table. The slightest variation in the angle of a player's shot will rapidly result in larger and larger variations in the following collisions between the pool balls. It has been said that to predict the outcome of your initial shot on this table, you would have to take into account the gravitational force exerted on the balls by a single electron at the edge of the galaxy.[8] Many dynamical systems exhibit this kind of chaotic behaviour. Although their basic components are deterministic (like the collisions between the pool balls), the behaviour of the systems is at least epistemically indeterministic: it is impossible to predict their future from a knowledge of their present states. Some authors claim that this epistemic unpredictability reflects an *ontological* indeterminism – the behaviour of even the macroscopic physical world is not fully determined by the laws of physics – though this claim is highly controversial.[9]

---

[7]Brian Cox and Jeff Forshaw, *The Quantum Universe: Everything That Can Happen Does Happen* (London: Penguin, 2012).

[8]James P. Crutchfield, J. Doyne Farmer, Norman H. Packard and Robert S. Shaw, 'Chaos', in Robert John Russell, Nancey Murphy and Arthur Peacocke (eds), *Chaos and Complexity: Scientific Perspectives on Divine Action*, 2nd ed. (Vatican City: Vatican Observatory/Berkeley, CA: Center for Theology and the Natural Sciences, 1997), pp. 35–48 (p. 37).

[9]For a brief discussion, see Polkinghorne, *Faith, Science and Understanding*, pp. 147–8.

Some science and theology authors believe that one or other of these theories leaves room for divine action where the older mechanistic view of the universe did not: God could act in the world to determine the outcome of quantum events, or perhaps chaotic processes. As we shall see, however, others are more sceptical.

In recent years, the divine action debate has become increasingly connected with debates about the theological problem of evil and suffering. If God *can* act in the world, why does God so often apparently *not* act to prevent the harm and suffering caused either by human wickedness or by natural causes?[10] The problem of evil will not be discussed further in this chapter, but will be taken up again in Chapter 3.

2.2 Defining the terms

The literature on divine action and modern science uses many specialized concepts, terms and acronyms, which can prove quite intimidating to newcomers to the discussion. Before we begin to engage with the literature, therefore, it might be helpful to introduce some of the key concepts and definitions. We should note, however, that these concepts, definitions and distinctions may not be neutral. Some of them reflect particular ways of framing the discussion and have certain assumptions built into them. These may tend to steer accounts of divine action in certain directions; as we shall see in later sections, some authors seek to change the direction of the debates by challenging some of these assumptions.[11]

Divine action is often classified into different types. The most basic distinction here is between *general* and *special* divine action, which has to do with whether God's actions interrupt the laws of

---

[10]For an influential discussion, see Philip Clayton and Stephen Knapp, *The Predicament of Belief: Science, Philosophy, and Faith* (Oxford: Oxford University Press, 2011), ch. 3. A central part of their solution is to confine divine action to interaction with human minds. For a critique (which nonetheless agrees on the importance of the problem of evil in the divine action debate), see Sarah Lane Ritchie, *Divine Action and the Human Mind* (Cambridge: Cambridge University Press, 2019), ch. 3.

[11]See Sarah Lane Ritchie, 'Dancing Around the Causal Joint: Challenging the Theological Turn in Divine Action Theories', *Zygon* 52, no. 2 (2017), pp. 361–79.

nature (Box 2.2). However, this raises the question of what we mean by 'laws of nature' (Box 2.2). A related issue, already hinted at in Section 2.1, is the issue of *determinism*, and whether divine action is compatible with deterministic physical laws (Box 2.3). Finally, divine action debates are largely about *causation*: In what sense (if any) does God cause events in the natural world? This clearly requires us to consider what we mean by causation, and whether we mean the same thing when referring to God and to created beings as 'causes' (Box 2.3).

BOX 2.2: DIVINE ACTION AND THE LAWS OF NATURE

Types of divine action

The literature often distinguishes between *general* and *special* divine action:

- *General divine action (GDA)*: Wesley Wildman defines this as 'the creation and sustaining of all reality in so far as this does not necessarily presume any specific providential divine intentions or purposes'.[12]

- *Special divine action (SDA)*: According to Wildman, SDA refers to 'specific providential acts, envisaged, intended, and somehow brought about in this world by God, possibly at particular times and places but possibly also at all times and places'.[13] It is often subdivided into:

  - *Interventionist SDA*, in which God suspends or overrules laws of nature;

  - *Non-interventionist SDA*: God does not interrupt the laws of nature, but works in and through them to bring about God's purposes.

---

[12]Wesley J. Wildman, 'The Divine Action Project, 1988–2003', *Theology and Science* 2, no. 1 (2004), pp. 31–75 (p. 37).
[13]Ibid.

Miracles are often (though not always) understood as interventionist SDAs.

Some authors distinguish between *objective* and *subjective* views of SDA:

- *Objective:* God's action brings about a change in the physical world;
- *Subjective:* the change occurs in the understanding of those who perceive the divine action.

Laws of nature

The distinctions between these types of divine action raise the question of what is meant by 'laws of nature'. Some authors distinguish between *laws of nature* and *laws of science:*

- *Laws of nature*: features of the natural world;
- *Laws of science*: scientific statements (such as Newton's laws of motion) which describe laws of nature more or less accurately.

Laws of nature (or science) may be understood in various ways:[14]

- *Necessitarian:* laws of nature are objective properties of the natural world which determine or constrain the course of events. They exist whether or not scientists have yet discovered or described them;
- *Regularist:* laws of nature are descriptions of regularities in natural systems or processes, which can be scientifically observed;
- *Instrumentalist:* strictly speaking, this refers to laws of science rather than nature. Instrumentalists see these laws as intellectual constructs, descriptions of the physical world which are successful in helping to organize

---

[14]See Saunders, *Divine Action and Modern Science*, pp. 60–72. These four ways represent the main options, though there are others that do not fit these categories exactly: for one account close, but not identical, to a regularist view, see Nancy Cartwright, *The Dappled World: A Study of the Boundaries of Science* (Cambridge: Cambridge University Press, 1999).

observations of nature into coherent and economical explanatory frameworks;

- *Probabilistic*: laws of nature state the probabilities of various events or outcomes, as the equations of quantum mechanics do.

BOX 2.3: DETERMINISM AND CAUSATION

Determinism and compatibilism

Determinism can be defined in various ways, but William Alston's definition of 'closed causal determinism' is fairly mainstream: 'every happening is uniquely determined to be just what it is by natural causes within the universe.'[15] What does this imply for divine action? Here the divine action debate has borrowed a distinction from philosophical discussions of human free will:

- *Compatibilism* is the view that SDA is compatible with fully deterministic physical processes;
- *Incompatibilism* denies that determinism is compatible with SDA: either some physical processes are indeterministic, or SDA cannot happen.

This distinction relates to the concept of a **causal joint**: some aspect of physical reality (e.g. an indeterministic physical process) which allows scope for an immaterial God to act on the material world.

Causation

Debates about divine action are largely about causation: What (or who) can cause events in the physical world? Two important sets of distinctions enter into these debates.

---

[15]William P. Alston, 'Divine Action, Human Freedom, and the Laws of Nature', in Robert John Russell, Nancey Murphy and C. J. Isham (eds), *Quantum Cosmology and the Laws of Nature: Scientific Perspectives on Divine Action*, 2nd ed. (Vatican City: Vatican Observatory/Berkeley, CA: Center for Theology and the Natural Sciences, 1999), pp. 185–206 (p. 187).

1) Primary and secondary causation: this is a distinction
    made by the mediaeval philosopher and theologian
    Thomas Aquinas.

    •   *Primary causation* refers to the causal agency of God,
        who is the ultimate cause of all things;
    •   *Secondary causes* are those attributed to created
        beings.

2) Material, formal, efficient and final causation, a set of
    distinctions originating with the ancient philosopher
    Aristotle (though he did not use this terminology):[16]

    •   *Material causation* has to do with the matter of
        which an object is made;
    •   *Formal causation* refers to the 'form' into which that
        matter is organized;
    •   *Efficient causation*: 'that from which the change …
        first begins.'[17] The physical cause and effect studied
        by modern science is (roughly speaking) efficient
        causation;
    •   *Final causation*: the end or purpose for which
        something happens.

Note that in Aristotelian thought, these are different kinds of
cause, which cannot be fully translated into one another. Broadly
speaking, modern science deals only with efficient causation, and
scientists sometimes assume this is the only kind there is in the
natural world. But Aristotle's fourfold scheme is a **metaphysical**
account, and science as such is not equipped to say whether or
not there is such a thing as final causation (for example) in the
natural world.

---

[16]Aristotle, *Metaphysics*, book 5, part 2, trans. W. D. Ross, online at http://classics.mit.
edu/Aristotle/metaphysics.5.v.html (accessed 16 January 2019). See Andrea Falcon,
'Aristotle on Causality', in Edward N. Zalta (ed.), *The Stanford Encyclopedia of
Philosophy* (Spring 2015 Edition), online at https://plato.stanford.edu/archives/spr2
015/entries/aristotle-causality/ (accessed 19 January 2019).
[17]Aristotle, *Metaphysics*, book 5, part 2.

Having defined some terms, how should we think about God's action in the world? As I suggested in Chapter 1, we can classify the various options by imagining a conversation about divine action between two voices: a scientific voice and a voice of the Christian tradition. Then the question becomes: What contribution should each voice make to our view of divine action in the world? As noted in Chapter 1, there are five possible answers.

2.3 Closing down the dialogue: Types 1 and 5

At either end of the scale are answers that effectively close down any dialogue by denying that one or other voice has anything to contribute.

2.3.1 Type 1: Only the scientific voice contributes

In the first type, only the scientific voice contributes, and the contribution of the Christian tradition is rejected or dismissed. This is the approach of those who believe, in the late Victor Stenger's words, that 'science shows that God does not exist'.[18] Though Stenger was a particle physicist and astronomer, his book *God: The Failed Hypothesis* ranges widely over topics that include evolution, neuroscience, cosmology, particle physics, the Bible and moral objections to religion. There is no space for a detailed response to the book – which is not without questionable assumptions, flawed logic, caricature and *non sequiturs* – but I can make a few general remarks.

---

[18]Victor J. Stenger, *God: The Failed Hypothesis – How Science Shows That God Does Not Exist* (Amherst, NY: Prometheus Books, 2007). Stenger, who died in 2014, was the author of numerous other works advocating scientific atheism, including *God and the Folly of Faith: The Incompatibility of Science and Religion* (Amherst, NY: Prometheus Books, 2012), *God and the Atom* (Amherst, NY: Prometheus Books, 2013) and *God and the Universe* (Amherst, NY: Prometheus Books, 2014).

Stenger aims to treat God's existence as a scientific hypothesis that makes testable predictions and can be shown to fail. He argues that if the God of Judaism, Christianity and Islam exists, this God's interactions with the cosmos and human life should have scientifically detectable effects. He makes a series of claims about what these effects should be, maintains that none of them has been detected and concludes that the cosmos is exactly as we should expect if this God did not exist.

One underlying assumption is that if God's action brings about effects in the world, it will be by the kind of efficient causation (see Box 2.3) that can be scientifically investigated. Stenger's target is, quite explicitly, the 'God of the gaps':[19] if natural causes can account for the way the world is, there is no evidence for God's existence (and Stenger thinks absence of evidence counts as evidence of absence). However, as we saw in Section 2.1, most science and theology scholars explicitly reject the God of the gaps. Many also argue that a God who is utterly **transcendent** (Box 2.4) cannot be thought of simply as a cause among other causes in the physical world. They therefore hold more complex views of causation in which divine and creaturely causes are not the same kind of cause (see Box 2.3). In such views, scientific evidence may be relevant to how we understand God's interaction with the world, but it will not be possible to treat divine action straightforwardly as a testable scientific hypothesis.

It is true, however, that during the history of modern science, God's action has often been conceived in much the same way that Stenger attacks. Moreover, some leading science and theology scholars do not make such a sharp distinction between divine and creaturely causation.[20] Some also seek to use scientific evidence to support the case for belief in God. Various scholars, for example, have argued that a method of 'inference to the best explanation' (IBE) points to the existence of God as the best explanation for a range of phenomena.[21] Though Stenger's critique certainly has

---

[19]Stenger, *God: The Failed Hypothesis*, pp. 13, 47, 126.
[20]For example, John Polkinghorne rejects the distinction between primary and secondary causation: see Section 2.5.4.
[21]For example, Arthur Peacocke, *Paths from Science towards God: The End of All Our Exploring* (Oxford: Oneworld, 2001); Polkinghorne, *Science and the Trinity*, p. 22.

its own weaknesses, it might sound a cautionary note about over-confidence in these kinds of **apologetic** strategy. On the other hand, dealing with Stenger's challenge by emphasizing the radical difference between divine and creaturely causation could lead to a type 5 position in which scientific knowledge is simply irrelevant to an understanding of divine action. As we shall see in later sections, many would find this equally unpalatable. The question of how scientific knowledge *should* influence an understanding of divine action lies at the heart of debates about the so-called Divine Action Project and the alternatives to it (Sections 2.4–2.6).

2.3.2 Type 5: Only the voice of the Christian tradition contributes

In the fifth type, only the voice of the Christian tradition contributes to theological understanding, and the contribution of the scientific voice is denied or dismissed. On some topics, this might mean denying the *validity* of certain scientific findings, as when young-earth creationists reject biological evolution (see Section 3.2.2). Probably more common, however, is the view that scientific insights about the physical world are valid but have no bearing on theological understanding.

A classic statement of this view is Stephen Jay Gould's proposal that science and religion are 'non-overlapping magisteria' (NOMA).[22] The magisterium of science covers the 'empirical realm': what the universe is made of and why it works the way it does. The religious magisterium governs 'ultimate meaning and moral value'.[23] Science and religion have authority in their own realms, but not in each other's.

Now, Gould does not want to close down the dialogue between science and religion. He emphasizes the closeness of the two magisteria and argues that 'respectful noninterference' should be 'accompanied by intense dialogue between the two subjects, each covering a central facet of human existence'.[24] However, the topic

---

[22]Gould, *Rocks of Ages.*
[23]Ibid., p. 6.
[24]Ibid., p. 5.

of this chapter – the divine action debate – brings to light the problematic nature of Gould's well-intentioned proposal.

The problems arise because the divine action debate is by definition concerned with God's relation to the empirical realm studied by science. If Christians claim that God acts in the material world, this inevitably raises questions about how God acts, what signs of God's action we can discern in the empirical realm and how we can discern them (though as we shall see, there are better and worse ways to ask these questions). From the perspective of NOMA, theological discussion of divine action in the physical world looks like an act of trespass into the magisterium of science.

However, the claim that God *does* act in the material world is at the heart of the Christian tradition, because Christian creeds and confessions affirm that the Son of God entered this material world in the form of a flesh-and-blood human being. Therefore, to rule out exploration of divine action in the physical world on NOMA grounds seems to be an unacceptable intrusion on the *religious* magisterium. In the divine action debate, the two magisteria unavoidably overlap. In short, the example of the divine action debate gives reasons to doubt that NOMA is a workable approach to theological engagement with then natural sciences, since it seems to prohibit claims to which Christian faith and theology are committed at their core. More generally, it is hard to see how any discussion of divine action in the physical world could get very far if it denied that scientific understandings of how the world works have any relevance whatsoever. In this debate at least, type 5 does not seem a viable alternative.[25]

If the two extreme positions in the typology are ruled out, the three middle positions remain to be considered.

2.4 The Divine Action Project: A candidate for type 2

From the late 1980s to the early 2000s, a major series of research conferences was sponsored jointly by the Vatican Observatory

---

[25]There may, however, be other areas in which more nuanced and limited versions of type 5 have something to be said for them: see Section 4.2.3.

and the Center for Theology and the Natural Sciences (CTNS) in Berkeley, California. Usually referred to as the Divine Action Project (DAP), it generated several edited volumes on topics ranging from quantum physics to neuroscience, all subtitled *Scientific Perspectives on Divine Action*.[26] The project has been massively important and influential, not only for the divine action debate but also for the whole science and theology field. In relation to divine action specifically, the definitions and distinctions summarized in Boxes 2.2 and 2.3 owe a great deal to the DAP, and it either generated or refined and developed many of the most influential accounts of divine action.

In terms of these definitions and distinctions (set in italics in this paragraph and the next two), the DAP focused more on *SDA* than *GDA*, because SDA was seen as more challenging in the context of modern science.[27] It was set up to allow what Philip Clayton called 'maximum traction' between theology and science. In practice, as Sarah Lane Ritchie has observed, this tended to mean critiquing theological claims scientifically – less often the reverse.[28] Most participants favoured *non-interventionist* SDA. They were (and are) reluctant to speak of God 'intervening' in natural processes, for various reasons:[29] divine intervention seems to undermine the intelligibility and regularity of the physical world, on which science depends; it seems inconsistent of God to interrupt the very laws that God has created; it intensifies the theological problem of evil, by raising the question why God so often does *not* seem to intervene to prevent innocent suffering.

Many participants (though not all) were *incompatibilists*, so to give an account of SDA, they had to show that certain natural processes were indeterministic in some ways: that nature is ontologically 'gappy'. In practice, this meant that much of the DAP was concerned with the search for *causal joints*.

---

[26]For an account of the DAP and an appraisal of its achievements, see Wildman, 'The Divine Action Project'. Details of the books and summaries of all the papers collected in them (ninety-one in total) are available online at http://www.ctns.org/books.html (accessed 17 January 2019).

[27]Wildman, 'The Divine Action Project', pp. 67–8, n. 9.

[28]Ritchie, *Divine Action and the Human Mind*, p. 8, citing Philip Clayton, *Adventures in the Spirit: New Forays in Philosophical Theology*, ed. Zachary Simpson (Minneapolis, MN: Fortress, 2008), pp. 53–4.

[29]Ritchie, 'Dancing Around the Causal Joint', pp. 363–4.

Many of those involved in the DAP claimed to be *regularists* about the laws of nature. Ritchie finds this surprising, since most were also non-interventionists. If laws of nature simply describe regularities (rather than prescribing what can and cannot happen), the interventionist/non-interventionist distinction dissolves. A description of the regularities of nature will simply include events caused by divine action, and it will be unnecessary to look for causal joints, or try and show how God can act without intervening in natural laws. So it seems inconsistent to identify as a regularist but still insist that divine action must be non-interventionist.[30]

Ritchie remarks that the overall effect of setting the DAP up in this way was to '[render] *science* as the final arbiter of whether and how God acts in nature; theology [was], thus, subjected to current scientific knowledge'.[31] This looks like a description of type 2 in my classification, though as we shall see later, some questions could be raised about this.

2.4.1 Quantum mechanics and divine action

The DAP included various specific proposals about causal joints or loci of divine action. The most popular was *quantum divine action*: the idea that God acts to determine the outcome of quantum events (such as the decay of radioactive nuclei) which would otherwise be indeterminate. One especially influential version of this has been Robert John Russell's theory of *quantum mechanical non-interventionist objective divine action* (QM-NIODA).[32]

Russell is modest about what a theory of SDA can achieve: 'we simply cannot answer the question of "how" God acts,' because 'God's causality is radically different from any of the kinds of

---

[30]Ibid., pp. 364–5. She uses the term 'descriptivist' instead of 'regularist'.

[31]Ibid., p. 366, emphasis in original.

[32]Robert John Russell, 'Divine Action and Quantum Mechanics: A Fresh Assessment', in Robert John Russell, Philip Clayton, Kirk Wegter-McNelly and John Polkinghorne (eds), *Quantum Mechanics: Scientific Perspectives on Divine Action* (Vatican City: Vatican Observatory/Berkeley, CA: Center for Theology and the Natural Sciences, 2001), pp. 293–328; Robert John Russell, 'Quantum Theory and the Theology of Non-Interventionist Objective Divine Action', in Philip Clayton (ed.), *The Oxford Handbook of Religion and Science* (Oxford: Oxford University Press, 2008), pp. 579–95.

causality we know about, just as God's nature as necessary being is ontologically different from ours as **contingent** being.'[33] He believes a theory of SDA must be non-interventionist, incompatibilist and objective. Divine action must also be understood as 'direct' rather than 'indirect' (not brought about simply as a consequence of some prior action of God), and 'mediated' rather than 'immediate' (God acts through natural processes). His own proposal, which he believes meets these requirements, is summarized in this way:

> God acts objectively and directly in and through (mediated by) quantum events to actualize one of several potential outcomes; in short, the collapse of the wave function occurs because of divine and natural causality working together even while God's action remains ontologically different from natural agency.[34]

Divine action, understood in this way, could influence the macroscopic world in various ways. For example, the radiation emitted by the decay of radioactive nuclei could cause genetic mutations which influenced the course of biological evolution.

Russell's theory requires causal gaps in nature, but he denies that this is a 'God of the gaps' theory of the sort that science and theology scholars object to. Rather, he claims that God has *created* nature to include causal gaps (to be 'ontologically indeterministic') at the quantum level. As we saw earlier (Box 2.1), there are various philosophical interpretations of quantum mechanics, not all of which see it as ontologically indeterministic. Russell therefore adopts a 'what if' approach: *if* quantum mechanics is ontologically indeterministic, then this is what we can say about divine action.

This kind of divine action would not be scientifically detectable or testable, because if quantum events are indeterministic, 'there is no natural cause for each specific quantum event for science to discover'.[35] Russell therefore does not see his proposal as a way to find scientific support for belief in God. He regards it instead as faith seeking understanding: an attempt to make rational sense, in dialogue with modern science, of a faith 'whose warrant

---

[33]Russell, 'Quantum Theory and the Theology of NIODA', p. 582.
[34]Ibid., p. 586.
[35]Ibid., p. 587.

and justification lie elsewhere, such as in Scripture, reason, and experience'.[36]

A number of others, including Nancey Murphy and Thomas F. Tracy, have adopted theories of quantum divine action similar to Russell's. These differ in some respects: for example, does God act in *all* quantum events (Murphy) or only in some (Tracy)?[37] Russell's answer to this question is that before conscious organisms evolved, God acted in all quantum events, but once conscious beings emerged, God 'increasingly refrain[ed]' from determining the outcomes of quantum events in their brains, in order to leave freedom for their conscious choices.[38]

2.4.2 Chaos theory and divine action

John Polkinghorne is unconvinced by theories of quantum divine action, and looks instead to chaos theory for the causal joint.[39] Polkinghorne holds a critically realist view of science in which 'epistemology models ontology'.[40] In other words, what we can know about the natural world reflects what it is really like. This leads him to argue that the epistemic unpredictability of chaotic systems reflects an ontological indeterminism. It is not only that we cannot *predict* the behaviour of these systems; they really *are not* fully determined by the laws of physics. Although the mathematical equations describing chaotic systems are fully deterministic, Polkinghorne believes that these equations are merely 'approximations to a more subtle and supple physical reality'.[41]

Polkinghorne speculates further about how this indeterminism might make a causal joint possible. He notes that the behaviour of chaotic systems is not completely haphazard: it includes order as well

---

[36]Ibid., p. 584.
[37]See Wildman, 'The Divine Action Project', p. 60.
[38]Russell, 'Quantum Theory and the Theology of NIODA', pp. 592–3.
[39]See, for example, John Polkinghorne, 'The Metaphysics of Divine Action', in Russell et al., *Chaos and Complexity*, pp. 147–56; also Polkinghorne, *Faith, Science and Understanding*, pp. 99–101, 121–5, 147–9.
[40]A frequent refrain of Polkinghorne's: for example, 'The Metaphysics of Divine Action', p. 148.
[41]Ibid., p. 153.

as disorder. The range of possible outcomes for any chaotic system is constrained within limits, which are described by a mathematical construct known as a *strange* (or *chaotic*) *attractor*.[42] According to Polkinghorne, the various pathways through a strange attractor are equal in energy, but different in the patterns of behaviour they represent. Because of this, an intentional agent could influence the behaviour of the system through the input of what he calls 'active information'.[43] He believes that this proposal can explain how human minds influence bodies, and how God acts in creation. The distinction between God and human creatures would be that God acts *purely* through active information, whereas the actions of humans (as embodied creatures) involve a mix of information and energy input.[44] Because this does not involve making changes to the matter or energy in the system, divine action is non-interventionist. Polkinghorne also emphasizes that it is top-down and holistic: God does not act merely through the 'clever manipulation of bits and pieces' of a chaotic system.[45]

2.4.3 Downward causation or whole-part constraint

Arthur Peacocke was one DAP participant who was sceptical about both quantum and chaos theory-based proposals for divine action.[46] According to his view of divine **omniscience**, if quantum events are truly random, even an all-knowing God can only predict their outcomes probabilistically: even God cannot know the outcome of any divine action at the quantum level. But if quantum events are really determined by hidden variables currently unknown to physics, then divine action to influence their outcome would be interventionist – which Peacocke, like most of the DAP, rules out. Likewise, he sees chaos theory as deterministic, so that divine action

---

[42]For an explanation of strange attractors, see Crutchfield et al., 'Chaos', pp. 37–44.

[43]Polkinghorne, 'The Metaphysics of Divine Action', p. 154.

[44]Polkinghorne, *Faith, Science and Understanding*, pp. 124–5.

[45]Polkinghorne, 'The Metaphysics of Divine Action', p. 154.

[46]Arthur R. Peacocke, 'God's Interaction with the World: The Implications of Deterministic "Chaos" and of Interconnected and Interdependent Complexity', in Russell et al., *Chaos and Complexity*, pp. 265–87 (pp. 276–82).

to influence outcomes of chaotic processes would be interventionist, even if humans could not predict those outcomes.

Peacocke's favoured model of divine action is sometimes described as 'top-down' or 'downward causation', though he prefers the term 'whole-part constraint'.[47] This is inspired by natural systems in which the state of the whole system influences the behaviour of its component parts. For example, convection in a heated liquid under certain circumstances can result in highly coordinated movement of its molecules.[48] One example from the biological world is the way evolutionary natural selection causes genetic changes in individuals.[49]

Peacocke argues that whole-part constraints like these can be models of God's interaction with the world. He maintains that the 'world-as-a-whole' can be regarded as a total system. Furthermore, he takes a **panentheistic** view of God's relationship with creation: the world-as-a-whole is '"in God," though ontologically distinct from God'.[50] This enables him to argue that

> God, by affecting the state of the world-as-a-whole, could … exercise constraints upon events in the myriad sub-levels of existence that constitute the 'world' without abrogating the laws and regularities that specifically pertain to them. … *Particular* events might occur in the world and be what they are because God intends them to be so, without at any point any contravention of the laws of [science].[51]

2.4.4 Other perspectives in the DAP

Quantum SDA, chaos theory and top-down or whole-part causation were three of the most influential proposals to emerge from the

---

[47]Ibid., pp. 272–6.
[48]Ibid., pp. 272–3.
[49]See Nancey Murphy, 'Avoiding Neurobiological Reductionism', in Juan José Sanguineti, Aribierto Acerbi and José Angel Lombo (eds), *Moral Behavior and Free Will: A Neurobiological and Philosophical Approach* (Morolo: If Press, 2011), pp. 201–22.
[50]Peacocke, 'God's Interaction with the World', p. 282.
[51]Ibid., p. 283, emphasis in original.

DAP. It is possible to adopt more than one of these proposals concurrently. For example, Nancey Murphy holds a version of the quantum SDA view, and she has also used ideas of top-down causation extensively, particularly in her work on neuroscience and theology.[52] Robert John Russell likewise emphasizes that his QM-NIODA theory 'is, at most, a proposal about one of many domains in nature where the effects of God's acts arise'.[53]

These were not the only views found within the DAP. A number of participants adopted a process theology perspective, which differs in important ways from classical **theism**.[54] The God of process theology is not the all-powerful, unchanging God who created the universe out of nothing. Instead, God is understood as 'dipolar'. As Niels Henrik Gregersen puts it, 'In one respect God is essentially unchangeable, but in another respect God is dependent on all that is encompassed by God.'[55] In a sense God is the Creator of the world – but 'God is also a creature of the world',[56] changed and affected by events in the world. In process theology, divine action may be thought of as a 'lure', which beckons the world towards a fuller realization of the good, but does not control or determine the outcomes of events.[57]

Others such as William Stoeger adopted a **Thomist** perspective, drawing particularly on Thomas Aquinas's distinction between primary and secondary causes (Box 2.3): God was understood as the primary cause, acting in the world through a wide variety of

---

[52]Nancey Murphy and Warren S. Brown, *Did My Neurons Make Me Do It? Philosophical and Neurobiological Perspectives on Moral Responsibility and Free Will* (Oxford: Oxford University Press, 2007).

[53]Russell, 'Quantum Theory and the Theology of NIODA', p. 592.

[54]For brief accounts of process thought in the context of science and theology, see Niels Henrik Gregersen, 'Three Varieties of Panentheism', and David Ray Griffin, 'Panentheism: A Postmodern Revelation', in Philip Clayton and Arthur Peacocke (eds), *In Whom We Live and Move and Have Our Being: Panentheistic Reflections on God's Presence in a Scientific World* (Grand Rapids, MI: Eerdmans, 2004), pp. 19–35 and 36–47 respectively.

[55]Gregersen, 'Three Varieties of Panentheism', p. 31; see also Griffin, 'Panentheism', pp. 43–4.

[56]Gregersen, 'Three Varieties of Panentheism', p. 31.

[57]Denis Edwards, *How God Acts: Creation, Redemption, and Special Divine Action* (Minneapolis, MN: Fortress, 2010), p. 61.

secondary causes.[58] This approach differs from the majority DAP
view on questions such as compatibilism *versus* incompatibilism,
and will be discussed more fully later. Finally, Wesley Wildman
and others rejected the idea of intentional divine action altogether.
Wildman identifies himself as a mystical theologian, who thinks of
'Ultimate Reality' as the ground of being, not as an 'agential being'
who acts in the world.[59]

2.4.5 Analysis and critique of the DAP

As I noted earlier, Sarah Lane Ritchie observes that the DAP
approach tends to subordinate theology firmly to science in
determining whether and how God acts in the world, which seems
to place the DAP as a whole within type 2.[60] I shall suggest later
(Section 2.5.5) that the picture may be more complex than this
suggests. However, the DAP certainly was deliberately set up to give
science considerable power to veto proposals about divine action.
This has enabled participants to critique each other's theories on
(apparently) scientific grounds. For example, John Polkinghorne
has often been sceptical about proposals for quantum SDA, while
numerous DAP participants have criticized his chaos theory-based
account. It also makes the entire project vulnerable to scientifically-
based criticism.

An extensive, detailed and technical critique of this sort, covering
all the main causal-joint proposals, comes from Nicholas Saunders.
To evaluate quantum SDA proposals, he considers a range of
interpretations of quantum theory (see Box 2.1) and asks what scope
each of them would allow for non-interventionist divine action.[61]
His answer is: little, if any. For example, in the 'Copenhagen'

---

[58]Ibid.

[59]Wildman, 'The Divine Action Project', pp. 32–3, 36; see also Wesley J. Wildman,
In Our Own Image: Anthropomorphism, Apophaticism, and Ultimacy (Oxford:
Oxford University Press, 2017).

[60]Ritchie, 'Dancing Around the Causal Joint', p. 366. Note, however, that Ritchie
still frames this as a question of the relationship between 'science' and 'theology',
whereas I have sought to re-frame it in terms of the weight given to scientific and
other sources *of* a theological understanding: see Section 1.5.

[61]Saunders, *Divine Action and Modern Science*, ch. 6.

interpretation, the only indeterminism in any system occurs at the point when it is measured or observed, so perhaps God acts to determine the outcome of otherwise undetermined measurement events. However, Saunders argues that the various possible accounts of how this could happen are either scientifically problematic or philosophically contradictory. The same is true of possibilities for divine action generated from other interpretations of quantum mechanics. He also finds them *theologically* problematic, because they are either likely to be interventionist (which the DAP tried to avoid) or they severely limit what God could achieve.[62]

Saunders is also sceptical about John Polkinghorne's chaos-based proposal.[63] He actually *defends* Polkinghorne against a frequent criticism that chaos theory is deterministic and therefore has no space for a causal joint. Saunders emphasizes that Polkinghorne is well aware of this, but (as we saw earlier) thinks that the deterministic mathematics of chaos only approximately reflects a more 'supple' and *indeterministic* physical reality. However, he shows that this distinction between the mathematics and physics of chaos creates other problems for Polkinghorne. One is that Polkinghorne's proposal requires different patterns of behaviour in a chaotic system to be equal in energy, so that 'active information' alone can influence the behaviour of the system without the input of energy. This is true in mathematical chaos theory, but Saunders argues there is no reason to think it is true of chaotic systems in the physical world.[64] He does not altogether rule out Polkinghorne's interpretation, but seems to find it very doubtful.[65]

Finally and more briefly, Saunders assesses Peacocke's model of whole-part causation. He considers it 'the most promising current theory', but thinks it still falls a long way short of a complete model of SDA.[66] His overall conclusion is that 'the prospects for supporting anything like the "traditional understanding" of God's activity in the world are extremely bleak ... *it is no real exaggeration to state that contemporary theology is in crisis*'.[67]

---

[62]Ibid., pp. 170–2.
[63]Ibid., pp. 173–206.
[64]For example, ibid., pp. 194–5.
[65]For example, ibid., p. 214.
[66]Ibid., p. 213.
[67]Ibid., p. 215, emphasis in original.

This conclusion has been widely rejected by DAP participants. For example, Wesley Wildman rejects Saunders's critique of quantum SDA proposals, while partly endorsing his criticisms of Polkinghorne.[68] Wildman's dispute with Saunders involves some quite technical argument about how the probabilistic laws of quantum mechanics are interpreted, which space does not permit me to explore here. In any event, the scientific detail and rigour of Saunders's critique make it a powerful challenge to the DAP, given the latter's aim of achieving 'maximum traction' (in Clayton's words) between science and theology.

Saunders shares this desire for 'traction': he believes that a satisfactory account of divine action must relate to a scientific understanding of the world, specifically enough to be tested for its consistency with that scientific understanding. His solution to the crisis is therefore to try harder.[69] However, another possible response to his diagnosis is summarized by Sarah Lane Ritchie. As we saw earlier, she notes that the DAP was set up in a way that gave science considerable power to challenge theological claims, but not vice versa. In recent years, increasing numbers of scholars have grown dissatisfied with this way of framing the discussion, and have become part of what she calls a 'theological turn'.[70]

2.5 The 'theological turn': A candidate for type 4

According to Ritchie, the theological turn is 'marked by a theological prioritization in articulating the basic relationship between God and the material world', a description that clearly suggests type 4 in my classification.[71] In this section, I shall survey three of Ritchie's examples – one Orthodox, one Pentecostal and one Catholic – and assess whether they do indeed reflect type 4.

---

[68]Wildman, 'The Divine Action Project', pp. 47–50, 55–7.
[69]Saunders, *Divine Action and Modern Science*, p. 216.
[70]Ritchie, 'Dancing Around the Causal Joint', p. 366.
[71]Ibid., pp. 366–7, with the caveat, as noted earlier, that Ritchie still frames this as a question about the relationship of 'science' to 'theology'.

2.5.1 Christopher Knight: A 'neo-Byzantine' model of divine action

The Orthodox theologian Christopher Knight is critical of the notion of non-interventionist divine action through causal joints, promoted by the DAP. This idea of divine action, he argues, fails to avoid the notion of God *interfering* with the world, but merely substitutes one kind of interference for another: God is no longer thought of as overruling the laws of nature, but using them as tools.[72] Knight is, however, indebted to some DAP participants – in particular, Arthur Peacocke – for aspects of the alternative view that he proposes. He shares with Peacocke a *panentheistic* view in which all of created reality is understood to be 'in some sense "in God" rather than separated from God',[73] and a 'theistic naturalism' in which God's purposes are worked out through the interplay of chance and necessity in natural processes. He also shares with Peacocke a 'sacramental view of matter'.[74] By this he means the view that all created things are 'naturalistically oriented toward God's ultimate intentions';[75] this is made particularly 'transparent' in the sacraments, where by God's grace, material things such as bread and wine disclose 'the genuine *nature* of creation'[76] – that is, how God intends it to be.

However, Knight's differences from Peacocke become more evident as he develops this view further, into what he calls an 'incarnational naturalism' and a 'neo-Byzantine model' of divine action.[77] The beginning of John's Gospel refers to the divine Word (*Logos*), through whom all things were made, who became flesh in Jesus (Jn 1.1-18). The *Logos* is understood as the reason and wisdom of God, which permeates and upholds the whole of creation. In that

---

[72]Christopher C. Knight, *The God of Nature: Incarnation and Contemporary Science* (Minneapolis, MN: Fortress, 2007), pp. 26–7.
[73]Ibid., p. 31.
[74]Ibid., p. 32, quoting Arthur Peacocke, *God and the New Biology* (London: Dent and Sons, 1986), p. 124.
[75]Knight, *The God of Nature*, p. 33.
[76]Ibid., p. 92, quoting Alexander Schmemann, *The Eucharist: Sacrament of the Kingdom* (Crestwood, NY: St Vladimir's Seminary Press, 1987), pp. 33–4, emphasis in original.
[77]Knight, *The God of Nature*, p. 111.

case, Knight argues, when the *Logos* became flesh in Jesus, this was not 'the sudden arrival of an otherwise absent *Logos*, but rather the completion of a process already begun in God's act of creation'.[78]

In this account, the *Logos* of God is at work in all creation. Knight explains this using the concept of the *logoi* in the thought of the seventh-century theologian Maximos the Confessor:

> Christ the creator *Logos* was understood ... to have implanted in every created thing, at the moment of its creation, a characteristic *logos* (a 'thought' or 'word') that manifests God's intention for the thing and constitutes its inner essence, making it distinctively itself and drawing it toward God.[79]

Knight argues that this account dissolves the distinction between GDA and SDA, because God is always active in creation through the *logoi*: there is no such thing as nature 'left to itself'.[80] However, the world as we experience it does not fully reflect God's purposes: it is **fallen**.[81] In Orthodox terms, this means that it is not fully 'natural', but '*subnatural*', displaying some 'opaqueness' to God's presence and purposes.[82] This 'opaqueness' is usually overcome only when humans respond to God in faith. Thus, the distinction between GDA and SDA should be replaced by a distinction between different *aspects of the world* and how God's purposes can be fulfilled in them. Some aspects of the world 'are, independently of the human response to God, still "transparent" enough for God's purposes to be fulfilled'; others 'are, so to speak, inoperative until [the human] response in faith is made'.[83] Even miracles should not be understood as God *interrupting* the laws of nature, but as 'manifestations of "laws of nature" that reflect, more fully than those laws of nature that are scientifically explorable, God's presence in all things'.[84]

---

[78]Stephen W. Need, 'Rereading the Prologue: Incarnation and Creation in John 1.1-18', *Theology* 106 (2003), pp. 397–404 (p. 403), quoted by Knight, *The God of Nature*, p. 96.
[79]Knight, *The God of Nature*, p. 98.
[80]Cf. ibid., p. 26.
[81]Ibid., pp. 86–95.
[82]Ibid., pp. 80, 90.
[83]Ibid., p. 94.
[84]Ibid.

2.5.2 Amos Yong: A Pentecostal-charismatic account

In his book *The Spirit of Creation*, Amos Yong offers a Pentecostal-charismatic account of divine action in critical dialogue with the DAP. Methodologically, he 'seek[s] to be constrained by the sciences in recognizing the limits of what can be said about divine action within the framework of modern science', but also to 'suggest how theological perspectives invite reconsideration of … **teleological** notions that have been by and large excluded from contemporary scientific discussion'.[85]

Yong offers a friendly but critical survey of the DAP, agreeing with Nicholas Saunders that its search for a causal joint has failed.[86] However, he identifies some key theological themes that have emerged from DAP discussions, including **Christology**, incarnation, **resurrection** and **eschatology**. He traces the ways in which these themes have been developed beyond the DAP by authors such as Peacocke, Polkinghorne and Russell. He then builds on their work to develop these themes further into what he calls a '**pneumatological** theology of eschatological divine action'.[87]

This account emphasizes that the acts of God seen in the life, death and resurrection of Jesus were the work of the Holy Spirit, and were a foretaste of the coming kingdom of God. This suggests various things. First, God promises a future transformation of creation – a 'new creation' – which cannot be predicted or extrapolated from current scientific knowledge. Second, this future transformation will also be the work of the Spirit. Third, in light of this, SDAs can be understood as 'charismatic actions of the Spirit that are … anticipations of the world to come … sign[s] of the new world that will be freed from the bondage of suffering and decay'.[88]

Yong defends a regularist view of the laws of nature (see Box 2.2), which means he does not need to see SDA or even

---

[85]Amos Yong, *The Spirit of Creation: Modern Science and Divine Action in the Pentecostal-Charismatic Imagination* (Grand Rapids, MI: Eerdmans, 2011), p. 73.
[86]Ibid., pp. 77–83.
[87]Ibid., pp. 83–101.
[88]Ibid., p. 93.

miracles as violations or interruptions of those laws.[89] Drawing on the philosophy of C. S. Peirce, he also argues that nature's laws can be seen as *teleological* – that is, directed towards goals or ends. '[F]or Peirce, the laws of nature are habitual tendencies that function teleologically like final causes.'[90] (On 'final causes', see Box 2.3.) Yong argues that this teleological view of the laws of nature supports his own eschatological view of divine action, which sees the Holy Spirit 'working in and through nature and its laws, but also ... transforming such in anticipation of the general shape of [God's] coming kingdom'.[91] This kind of future-oriented divine action is not scientifically measurable or testable; it can only be discerned from the standpoint of the future (as it were), 'from the perspective of Christ's inaugurating the kingdom'.[92]

2.5.3 Denis Edwards: A neo-Thomist perspective

The Catholic theologian Denis Edwards takes further the approach that William Stoeger developed in the DAP, understanding divine action in terms of Thomas Aquinas's distinction between primary and secondary causes (see Box 2.3).[93] Edwards develops this approach in a nuanced and sophisticated way, heavily influenced by the twentieth-century Catholic theologian Karl Rahner. He maintains that a Christian theology of divine action must be 'grounded in ... the central conviction of [the Christian] tradition, that God has acted to bring salvation to the world in the life, death and resurrection of Jesus and in the outpouring of the Spirit'.[94]

---

[89]Ibid., pp. 112–18.
[90]Ibid., p. 124.
[91]Ibid., p. 125.
[92]Ibid., p. 97.
[93]Edwards, *How God Acts*, p. 61. The word 'Thomist' in the section heading refers to the thought of the mediaeval philosopher-theologian Thomas Aquinas. In some contexts, 'neo-Thomism' specifically refers to the nineteenth-century revival of Aquinas's thought in official Catholic teaching. However, in the science and theology field, it is often used in a looser sense to describe theological perspectives that draw on Aquinas's thought in new and creative ways.
[94]Edwards, *How God Acts*, p. 1.

However, it must also be 'faithful … to the world we actually encounter', which means being 'shaped by the best insights of the sciences'.[95] Throughout Edwards's account – more than in many discussions of divine action – questions in science and theology are strongly connected to the New Testament's witness to Jesus Christ and the Christian tradition's reflection on that witness.

Edwards was a participant in the DAP, and shares its aim to give an objective, non-interventionist account of SDA. As we have seen, the way he attempts to do this is to use Aquinas's distinction between God's causal agency (primary causation) and the secondary causes that operate in the created world. Edwards finds this distinction attractive because it emphasizes the radical difference between God's causal agency and that of creatures.[96] God is the transcendent Creator on whom everything depends for its existence. Creatures are finite, and can only be causal agents because the Creator gives them this capacity. This distinction between divine and creaturely causation was sometimes obscured in the DAP, when some participants treated God's action more or less as a cause among other causes in the physical world.[97]

Another reason Edwards is attracted to Aquinas's idea of primary and secondary causes is that it shows how 'God gives creatures independence and integrity, including the capacity to act as real causes'; in this way, 'God … respects the autonomy of creation.'[98] Indeed, he presses this thought further than Aquinas. In Aquinas's account, God generally acts through secondary causes but may act 'immediately', without the mediation of secondary causes.[99] Edwards, on the other hand, seems to consider SDA *only* through secondary causes. Even miracles, he thinks, can be seen in this way: as 'wonderful manifestations of the Spirit that occur *through*

[95]Ibid.
[96]Ibid., p. 63.
[97]William R. Stoeger, 'The Divine Action Project: Reflections on the Compatibilism/ Incompatibilism Divide', *Theology and Science* 2, no. 2 (2004), pp. 192–6 (p. 193).
[98]Edwards, *How God Acts*, p. 62.
[99]Thomas Aquinas, *Summa Theologiae*, trans. Fathers of the English Dominican Province, 2nd ed. (1920), 1a, q. 105, arts. 2, 6. Online at http://www.newadvent.org/ summa/1105.htm (accessed 20 July 2018).

secondary causes'.[100] To support this view, he adopts a regularist view of the laws of nature (see Box 2.2). He also takes up Stoeger's idea that there may be laws of nature which we do not, and perhaps cannot, understand scientifically. Thus, 'miracles may occur through a whole range of secondary causes that our current science cannot yet model.'[101] Moreover, for the Bible and Christian theology, the important thing about miracles is not that they suspend the laws of nature, but that they are 'signs and manifestation [sic] of God's saving action'.[102] They occur in particular historical contexts and their purpose is to excite wonder and inspire faith and trust in God.

Edwards explores the potential of this view that God acts in a non-interventionist way through secondary causes, for a range of theological themes. He even argues that the resurrection of Jesus can be understood in this way.[103] This is where his account shows some signs of strain. In order to maintain this view of the resurrection, he focuses on the Christian community's experience of the risen Christ, the resurrection appearances to the first disciples and the implications of the resurrection for the future transformation of the whole creation. Certainly, these are all theologically important aspects of the resurrection message. But Edwards explicitly sidesteps the accounts of Jesus's empty tomb in all four Gospels, which would present a tougher challenge to his claim that the resurrection 'can be understood as God acting through secondary causes'.[104]

2.5.4 The theological turn: Analysis and critique

The theological turn and some of the key ideas involved in it have attracted criticisms of various kinds. For example, as well as specific criticisms of particular theological-turn proposals, Sarah Lane Ritchie has two main general concerns.

---

[100]Edwards, *How God Acts*, p. 84, emphasis in original. Cf. Aquinas, *Summa Theologiae*, 1a, q. 105, arts. 7, 8, where miracles are said to be 'outside the course of nature' and to 'surpass the power of nature'.
[101]Edwards, *How God Acts*, p. 87.
[102]Ibid.
[103]Ibid., pp. 91–106.
[104]Ibid., p. 100.

First, 'does the theological turn ... actually address the problem of the causal joint?'[105] Theological-turn authors, of course, would deny that they need to address this problem. They would regard the search for a causal joint as wrong-headed, because it mistakenly assumes that there could be such a thing as nature *without* God's (special) involvement – nature 'left to itself', as Christopher Knight puts it.[106] Ritchie, though, still thinks that we need an account of how the 'transcendent, immaterial' God interacts with the material world. Otherwise, we will fail to do justice to God's **transcendence** (Box 2.4): without some kind of causal joint, 'God would be less than God, part of the physical world itself'.[107]

However, care is needed in framing this issue. The word 'immaterial' could, if we are not careful, lead us to imagine a God who is somehow less substantial than physical beings, though I am certainly not suggesting this is what Ritchie intends. Likewise, some accounts of divine action can give the impression that the transcendent Creator has *fewer* possibilities than created beings for acting in the world. John Polkinghorne's proposal that humans may act in the world through inputs of either energy or 'active information', whereas God only acts through the latter, is a case in point.[108] Ritchie may be right that we need to think more about how a transcendent God, who is ultimate Reality, interacts with God's material creation. However, if we frame that thinking as a question about the causal joint, it may be at risk of the same problems as the causal-joint proposals in the DAP – which Ritchie herself criticizes.

Theological-turn authors might reply that their accounts offer resources for doing this thinking in more helpful ways than causal-joint talk. For example, as Ritchie acknowledges, Knight's perspective can make use of the Orthodox distinction between the divine 'essence' and 'energies' to give an account of God's transcendence and **immanence** (Box 2.4).[109] Also, both Knight and Denis Edwards in different ways use the concept of primary and

[105]Ritchie, 'Dancing Around the Causal Joint', p. 377.
[106]Knight, *The God of Nature*, p. 26.
[107]Ritchie, 'Dancing Around the Causal Joint', p. 377.
[108]Polkinghorne, *Faith, Science and Understanding*, pp. 124–5.
[109]Ritchie, 'Dancing Around the Causal Joint', pp. 373–4; Christopher C. Knight, 'An Eastern Orthodox Critique of the Science-Theology Dialogue', *Zygon* 51, no. 3 (2016), pp. 573–91 (p. 584).

secondary causation (Box 2.3) to distinguish between God's action and the action of created beings.

BOX 2.4: DIVINE TRANSCEND-ENCE AND IMMANENCE

Christian theology (like some other faith traditions) often uses the language of divine *transcendence* to express the fundamental distinction between the Creator and the creation. God is not merely a being *within* the cosmos, but transcends or goes 'beyond' the limits of the whole created universe. Transcendence is (in a sense) the opposite of divine *immanence*, the idea that God is present always and everywhere in God's creation.

Mainstream Christian theology insists that God is *both* utterly transcendent *and* fully immanent. Various different ways of expressing this have played a part in divine action debates. One is Aquinas's distinction between primary and secondary causes (Box 2.3). Another is the Orthodox distinction between God's *essence* and *energies*, which has some influence on Christopher Knight's Orthodox account of divine action. This distinction was formulated by the Orthodox theologian Gregory Palamas (1296–1359). 'Essence' refers to God's being as God really is, which cannot be known or comprehended by human creatures. 'Energies' refers to the activity of God in the created world, which can be known and experienced by humans.[110]

This, however, brings us to Ritchie's second concern: whether the theological turn 'take[s] science seriously enough'.[111] Theological-turn authors often claim that God causes events in the world in ways that are undetectable *in principle* by science. For example (as we have seen), some argue that God is the primary cause of events in the world, acting through secondary causes (Box 2.3).

---

[110]See John Meyendorff, *Byzantine Theology: Historical Trends and Doctrinal Themes,* 2nd ed. (New York: Fordham University Press, 1983), pp. 180–90.
[111]Ritchie, *Dancing Around the Causal Joint,* p. 377.

Science can only investigate the secondary causes. Ritchie endorses John Polkinghorne's complaint that this is 'an unintelligible kind of theological doublespeak'.[112] Put more generally, such accounts may be entirely compatible with scientific knowledge, but because they claim that science cannot in principle investigate God's activity, they are insulated from scientific criticism. Echoing Philip Clayton, Ritchie complains that they completely reject 'traction between science and religion',[113] and the cost of this is that they fail to engage with scientific understandings of the world.[114]

2.5.5 Divine Action Project versus theological turn?

Ritchie depicts a confrontation between the DAP and the theological turn: theological-turn authors 'share a commitment to explicitly theological frameworks for divine action, and this is in direct opposition to the standard divine action theories drawing upon supposedly underdetermined aspects of the natural world'.[115] As already noted, this seems to place the DAP in type 2 of my classification, and the theological turn in type 4.

However, the picture may be more complex than this. Certainly, some DAP participants have understood their work in a way I would identify as type 2. Arthur Peacocke, for example, saw his academic project as an attempt to re-establish the credibility of theology in the face of the robust challenge from modern science. He believed that in order to meet that challenge theology would have to adopt

---

[112]John Polkinghorne, *Science and Christian Belief: Theological Reflections of a Bottom-Up Thinker* (London: SPCK, 1994), pp. 81–2; Ritchie, *Dancing Around the Causal Joint*, p. 370.

[113]Ritchie, *Dancing Around the Causal Joint*, p. 377.

[114]This might suggest that the primary/secondary cause distinction is an example of type 5, an approach in which scientific investigation of secondary causes is valid in its own sphere, but has nothing to contribute to a theological understanding of how God, as primary cause, acts. Yet this is clearly not how authors like Edwards (Section 2.5.3) or Stoeger (Section 2.6) intend the distinction to be used. They think that since God as primary cause acts in the world *through* secondary causes, science can tell us something about this action of God, even if there must ultimately be an element of mystery about the relationship between primary and secondary causes.

[115]Ibid., p. 376.

methods and criteria more like those of science.[116] Robert John Russell understands his work very differently. In a recent account, he has described it as

> part of a general constructive theology ... whose warrant and justification lie elsewhere, such as in Scripture, reason, and experience, and which incorporates the results of science and the concerns for nature into its broader framework mediated by philosophy.[117]

Russell is modest about the scope of divine action theories, including his own. He emphasizes the radical difference between divine and creaturely causation, and the limits on what science can tell us about divine action.[118] The broader framework he advocates for the science–theology relationship is one of 'Creative Mutual Interaction' (CMI), in which science can influence theology in various ways, but there are also ways theology can influence science.[119] Both this broad framework and Russell's specific comments about his own theory of divine action resemble type 3 more than type 2.

Despite this, as Ritchie suggests, it does look as though the central questions in the DAP were framed in a way that pushed the project as a whole towards type 2, even if that did not reflect everyone's broader theological aims. However, not all DAP participants accepted this framing. As we shall see in the next section, William Stoeger was one who tried to reformulate some key aspects of the DAP, in a way that would create space for something like a type 3 account.[120]

From the other side, there may also be more continuity between the DAP and the theological turn than Ritchie suggests. As we have seen, all the examples of the theological turn surveyed in this section are indebted to the DAP and show significant continuities with it. Moreover, how far *does* the theological turn really privilege theology over science? Recall that an author such as Yong 'seek[s] to be

---

[116]Peacocke, 'Science and the Future of Theology', pp. 119–40.

[117]Russell, 'Quantum Theory and the Theology of NIODA', p. 584.

[118]Ibid., p. 582.

[119]See Russell and Wegter-McNelly, 'Science and Theology', pp. 19–34 (esp. pp. 33–4).

[120]See Stoeger, 'The Divine Action Project', pp. 192–6.

constrained by the sciences' in speaking about divine action, as well as 'suggest[ing] how theological perspectives invite reconsideration' of ideas sidelined by contemporary science.[121] In short, just how sharp has the 'theological turn' been so far? Perhaps a more thoroughgoing type 4 account of divine action, more fully matching Ritchie's description of the theological turn, has yet to be written.

2.6 Middle ground in the divine action debate: Type 3

We have seen how the DAP and the more recent 'theological turn' in the divine action debate share more common ground than they appear to at first sight, but as Ritchie suggests, the way the DAP was framed tended to turn it into a largely type 2 exercise. However, I have also noted that not everyone accepted this framing wholesale. One major DAP participant who did not was the astrophysicist and Catholic theologian William Stoeger.

One of Stoeger's DAP contributions states the aim of 'taking seriously both revelation and the knowledge of reality we have from the sciences ... letting these two areas of our knowledge critically interact and dialogue with each other'.[122] For him, this means adopting the Thomist distinction between primary and secondary causation. God, as primary cause of all things, is radically different from all other 'entities, causes and agents we are familiar with' – a principle Stoeger labels the 'protocol against idolatry'.[123] He takes a regularist view in which so-called laws of nature are 'the regularities, processes, structures and relationships which we find in reality',[124] which 'are as they are by God's allowance and choice'.[125]

---

[121]Yong, *The Spirit of Creation*, p. 73.
[122]William R. Stoeger, 'Describing God's Action in the World in Light of Scientific Knowledge of Reality', in Russell et al., *Chaos and Complexity*, pp. 239–61 (p. 261).
[123]Stoeger, 'The Divine Action Project', p. 193.
[124]William R. Stoeger, 'Conceiving Divine Action in a Dynamic Universe', in Robert John Russell, Nancey Murphy and William R. Stoeger (eds), *Scientific Perspectives on Divine Action: Twenty Years of Challenge and Progress* (Vatican City: Vatican Observatory/Berkeley, CA: Center for Theology and the Natural Sciences, 2008), pp. 225–47 (p. 237).
[125]Stoeger, 'Describing God's Action in the World', p. 248.

He emphasizes the distinction between 'our laws of nature' (our partial and provisional knowledge of nature's regularities) and '"the laws" in themselves'.[126] Divine actions which appear to violate the laws of nature might actually be consistent with 'higher laws': natural regularities and relationships which science does not – perhaps cannot – know about.[127]

In light of this, Stoeger critiques and seeks to re-frame some of the DAP's key definitions and distinctions. One is the interventionist/ non-interventionist distinction. While he agrees with most DAP participants that interventionist divine action would be theologically problematic, he points out that '[w]hat counts as an intervention is obviously relative to what [the laws of nature] actually are'.[128] If 'the laws of nature' as they really are include regularities, relationships and processes that science cannot fully understand, it may be impossible to say whether certain divine actions are interventionist or not.

Stoeger also seeks to re-frame the distinction between compatibilism and incompatibilism. As a regularist, he rejects the idea of 'rigid physical determinism in nature',[129] in which case it is beside the point to ask whether or not divine action would be compatible with deterministic natural processes. Stoeger argues that what is really at stake here is the difference between divine and creaturely causation. Incompatibilists, whether or not they mean to, fail to emphasize the radical difference between God's action and the actions of creatures,[130] a distinction he thinks it is vital to maintain. Finally, his understanding of the laws of nature and of primary and secondary causation has led him to re-frame the distinction between SDA and GDA. Taking up an idea from Thomas Tracy, he argues that SDA 'should not be separated from God's universal

---

[126]Stoeger, 'Conceiving Divine Action', p. 237. See also William R. Stoeger, 'Contemporary Physics and the Ontological Status of the Laws of Nature', in Russell et al., *Quantum Cosmology and the Laws of Nature*, pp. 207–31.

[127]Stoeger, 'Conceiving Divine Action', pp. 237–8.

[128]Stoeger, 'The Divine Action Project', p. 194.

[129]Ibid., p. 195.

[130]Note, however, that in recent writings, Robert Russell, an incompatibilist whose account of quantum SDA was discussed as an example of type 2, has also emphasized the radical difference between divine and creaturely causation: Russell, 'Quantum Theory and the Theology of NIODA', p. 582.

creative action, but rather considered as a particular manifestation or mode of that divine creative action, more broadly conceived'.[131]

In a different way from Stoeger, Sarah Lane Ritchie also appears to be calling for a type 3 approach. As we have seen, she accepts the key criticisms levelled by theological-turn authors at the DAP and its search for the causal joint. Yet she also criticizes the theological turn for not taking science seriously enough. In effect she calls for an approach to divine action that will retain the gains of the theological turn, but still allow for 'traction' between science and theology. In her view, this must mean giving an account of the causal joint. One question this raises is how this new kind of causal-joint discussion will be different from the DAP approach that she criticizes: How will the approach she advocates avoid replicating the problems she finds with the DAP?

2.7 Conclusion

The divine action debate has been the first test case for my proposed typology. First, I examined the two extreme positions, which would rule out any interaction between the voices of scientific disciplines and the Christian tradition in shaping theological understanding. One was the scientific atheism represented by Victor Stenger, which I concluded has serious enough flaws that it can be set aside. The other was the view that scientific perspectives may be valid, but are irrelevant to theological understanding. This view may seem to be warranted by Stephen Jay Gould's position that science and religion are 'non-overlapping magisteria' (NOMA), but a brief examination of the NOMA view showed it to be unworkable in the divine action debate.

Much of the chapter was concerned with the DAP and its critics. We saw how, according to Sarah Lane Ritchie, the DAP makes 'science ... the final arbiter of whether and how God acts in nature'.[132] She contrasts this with the so-called theological turn, which gives *theology* the priority in 'articulating the basic

---

[131]Stoeger, 'Conceiving Divine Action', p. 244.
[132]Ritchie, 'Dancing Around the Causal Joint', p. 366, emphasis in original.

relationship between God and the material world'.[133] This would seem to place the DAP and the theological turn in types 2 and 4, respectively. However, the picture is more complex than that. The majority DAP approach does indeed resemble type 2, but some DAP contributors and at least some examples of the theological turn are closer to type 3. A classification that includes the three central types of my scheme helps to make this clear. Perhaps also the guiding question of my typology lends itself to a more fine-grained analysis of the positions. The question usually asked by commentators on the DAP is whether 'science' or 'theology' takes priority in an account of divine action. My question instead asks how scientific findings and theories function as a *source* of theology in dialogue with other sources, notably Scripture and tradition. This question invites us to attend closely to the nuances of *how* scientific insights are shaping different authors' understandings of the world and ourselves in relation to God. It also invites us to consider how scientific insights *should* (and should not) shape such an understanding.

In relation to that last question – how scientific insights *should* shape theological understanding – I have agreed with Ritchie and others that the dominant (type 2) DAP approach places unwelcome restrictions on a Christian vision of how God acts in the world. In this debate at least, type 2 seems to have significant drawbacks as a way of relating the contributions that science and the Christian tradition make to theological understanding. Type 3 approaches – those of Stoeger and others and the one to which Ritchie points – allow more scope for the Christian tradition to speak in its own characteristic voice. Yet I suggested that the kind of type 3 account Ritchie advocates (at any rate) is in danger of drifting back towards type 2 and the same problems that she finds in the DAP. I also hinted that there may be a need for a *sharper* theological turn than in the examples Ritchie and I survey: one that more clearly represents my type 4.

Such an approach would begin by asking how we should speak of God's action in the world in the context of a Christian theological tradition with its roots in the Bible. It would then ask how modern scientific understandings might relate to that biblically

---

[133]Ibid., p. 367.

and theologically formed view, and how they might be critically appropriated so as to inform and enrich it.

The main cost of this approach would be the loss of 'traction' between science and theology. For this reason, not only DAP participants but also a DAP critic like Ritchie would very likely accuse it of failing to take science seriously enough. Up to a point, those taking a type 4 approach need not be too troubled by this critique, since they would see the quest for traction as part of the problem with the way the DAP was set up. On their view, we just misunderstand the nature and methods of theology if we think that theological claims could be assessed scientifically in the way many DAP participants hoped for. The kind of traction sought by the DAP is not something that theology *ought* to learn from science. However, Ritchie's critique does signal a danger that such scholars ought to take seriously. This is the risk that a theologically shaped account might become altogether disconnected from scientific insights and perspectives, drifting from type 4 into type 5.

In summary, I have tentatively suggested that types 3 and 4 both offer scope for a rich theological engagement with scientific voices on questions about God's action in the world. However, each of these types of approach is at risk of drifting towards one of the more problematic types (2 and 5 respectively). It also seems that those representing types 3 and 4 are particularly well placed to draw attention to each other's characteristic dangers: to see the specks – or perhaps the logs – in each other's eyes (cf. Mt. 7.3-5).

3

The problem of natural evil after Darwin

CHAPTER SUMMARY

My second test case is one of the toughest challenges that evolutionary biology poses for Christian theology: a particular form of the problem of **natural evil**. Biological evolution by natural selection (see Box 3.1) generates rich and diverse new forms of life through a process that depends on 'disvalues' such as suffering, death and species extinction. If the cosmos and all living beings are God's creation (as Christians affirm), this seems to suggest that God either willed these evolutionary disvalues or was powerless to prevent them. Evolutionary suffering and destruction therefore call into question God's power, goodness or both. How (if at all) is it possible to speak of an all-powerful, perfectly good God in the face of evolutionary evil?[1]

In this chapter I survey various answers to that question, classified according to the five types in my scheme (see Chapter 1, 'Chapter Summary'). First I briefly deal with examples of the two extreme types:

Type 1: Richard Dawkins's view that this is exactly the kind of universe we should expect if there were no God; one in which meaningless suffering and meaningless good fortune occur randomly.

---

[1]Some of the material in this chapter was previously published in Neil Messer, 'Evolution and Theodicy: How (Not) to do Science and Theology', *Zygon* 53, no. 3 (2018), pp. 821–35.

Type 5: the young-earth creationist view, which acknowledges the seriousness of the problem of evil posed by evolution, and takes this as one reason (among others) to reject evolutionary biology.

I argue that both these responses, as well as closing down any dialogue between scientific and Christian voices, have major shortcomings of their own and can be set aside as serious options.

I then consider examples of the middle three positions in my classification.

Type 2 is represented by two contrasting accounts:

- Ruth Page's argument that if we think of God as 'making and doing', this makes God responsible for natural evil on a colossal scale. She proposes instead that God creates the possibility for things to exist and events to happen, and 'companions' all beings as their possibilities unfold, but does nothing to direct *how* they unfold.

- Wesley Wildman's proposal that God should not be thought of as a personal God with humanly recognizable characteristics like goodness, but as the 'ground of being' who is the basis of all cosmic possibilities, good and evil alike.

Type 3 focuses on Christopher Southgate's 'compound theodicy', which consists of the following arguments:

- An evolutionary process with all its disvalues is the only (or at any rate the best) way even an all-powerful God could create a world with complex life;

- God suffers along with God's creatures;

- God promises an **eschatological** future in which the 'victims' of evolution will be ultimately fulfilled and compensated for their suffering;

- Humans are called to work with God here and now for the 'healing' of evolutionary suffering.

Type 4 includes two contrasting approaches:

- Accounts by Nicola Hoggard Creegan and myself, which in different ways identify evolutionary suffering as an aspect of evil, something *not* willed by God. The origin and explanation of this natural evil are ultimately a mystery, but it will be finally overcome in God's promised good future.

- Henri Blocher's argument that natural evil and suffering in the present world result from the **original sin** of a historical Adam and Eve; there was no natural evil in the world prior to the evolution of humans and their **fall** into sin.

Comparison of Wildman's type 2 and Southgate's type 3 approaches reveals basic differences about the task and nature of theology. Southgate in effect sees theology as an exercise in faith seeking understanding. From that perspective, the theological cost of an account like Wildman's may seem too high, even though Southgate praises Wildman's honesty and incisiveness. In its basic theological commitments, Southgate's approach has more in common with a type 4 approach like mine, but we differ about how much, and what kind of thing, theology ought to learn from the natural sciences.

The analysis of these debates bears out the main conclusions of Chapter 2: type 2 approaches have significant drawbacks; types 3 and 4 are more satisfactory approaches to the engagement of theology with the natural sciences; but both these types have their own characteristic dangers, and each is well placed to draw attention to the dangers of the other. A further conclusion, emerging more clearly in this chapter than Chapter 2, is that each type in the typology may include widely differing, and even opposing, accounts. This is because the typology is concerned with methods and approaches rather than the substance of the conclusions.

3.1 Introduction

In a frequently quoted passage, the philosopher of biology David Hull pithily expressed the theological problem of natural evil posed by Darwinian evolution:

What kind of God can one infer from the sort of phenomena epitomized by the species on Darwin's Galápagos Islands? The evolutionary process is rife with happenstance, **contingency,** incredible waste, death, pain and horror. ... Whatever the God implied by evolutionary theory and the data of natural history may be like, He is not the Protestant God of waste not, want not. He is also not a loving God who cares about His productions. He is not even the awful God portrayed in the book of Job. The God of the Galápagos is careless, wasteful, indifferent, almost diabolical. He is certainly not the sort of God to whom anyone would be inclined to pray.[2]

Like many others, Hull suggests that Darwinian evolution (see Box 3.1) poses a particular problem for Christian belief in an all-powerful, perfectly good Creator. It is not just that pain, suffering, death and destruction are widespread in the natural world, which was of course well known before Darwin's time. The problem posed by Darwin is that the same evolutionary processes that have generated all living things, including our own species, have also given rise to much of the violence, suffering and destruction that we experience and see around us. **Pathogenic** microorganisms, for example, are products of the same evolutionary processes as we are, and the disease processes which cause suffering and death to their hosts represent successful evolutionary strategies for those microorganisms.

BOX 3.1: DARWINIAN AND
NEO-DARWINIAN EVOLUTION

Darwin, Wallace and natural selection

It is hardly possible to overstate the importance of Charles Darwin's (1809–82) evolutionary theory to modern biology. Darwin, however, did not invent the idea of evolution: by his time, scientific evidence was accumulating that living species change over time, and some well-known accounts of evolution (or 'transmutation', as it was then generally called) had already been published. Darwin's major contribution was a convincing account of how evolutionary change could take place: the theory

---

[2]David L. Hull, 'The God of the Galápagos', *Nature* 352 (1991), pp. 485–6.

of *natural selection*, also developed independently by Alfred Russel Wallace (1823–1913).

Darwin's idea was that there is a 'struggle for existence' between members of the same species and population. For example, they may be in competition for scarce food, or under threat from predation. Individuals in the population will vary in many ways, and some of these variations may equip some individuals to do better than others in the struggle for existence. They may for instance be better able to access food or escape predators. Those individuals will have a greater chance of surviving long enough to reproduce, so the variations they carry will be more likely to be passed on to future generations. Over many generations, if the same 'selection pressures' in the environment persist, the characteristics of the successful individuals will become more frequent and more pronounced in the population.

The Modern Synthesis and molecular biology

Darwin's theory, though groundbreaking, was incomplete. In particular, Darwin could not give an account of *how* variations could be passed on to future generations. Unknown to him, around the same time the Austrian monk Gregor Mendel (1822–84) was conducting the experiments on inheritance in pea plants which would lay the foundations of modern genetics. Research in population genetics from the 1920s to the 1940s showed that Mendelian genetics could fill this gap in Darwinian evolutionary theory. The combination of these theories was dubbed the 'modern synthesis' by Julian Huxley,[3] and is often also known as 'neo-Darwinism'.

The discipline of molecular biology began in the 1930s, and advanced rapidly from the 1950s onwards, with groundbreaking research into the molecular structures of DNA, proteins and other biological molecules. The growth of molecular biology made great contributions to the understanding of evolution in many ways. Evolutionary change could now be studied not only at the level of the visible structures and functions of organisms but at the level of the genetic information encoded in DNA and its effects on molecular structures and processes in living cells.

---

[3]Julian Huxley, *Evolution: The Modern Synthesis* (London: Allen and Unwin, 1942).

Moreover, violence, suffering and destruction are often the *means* by which new forms of life evolve. Predation illustrates this powerfully: as Holmes Rolston put it, 'The cougar's fang has carved the limbs of the fleet-footed deer, and vice versa.'[4] The features of the cougar's body, brain and behaviour that make it so well equipped to hunt and kill create an evolutionary selection pressure on its prey to develop bodies, brains and behaviours that are finely adapted to escape their predators, and those features in turn create a selection pressure on the predators to develop ever more effective means of hunting and killing. Those cougars that are not successful enough at catching prey may starve, along with their young, and those deer that are not successful enough at escaping their predators will die a painful death.

Authors differ about *which* features of the evolutionary process (if any) raise a theological problem of natural evil.[5] Hull, as we have seen, identifies 'happenstance, contingency, incredible waste, death, pain and horror'. Others do not see happenstance, contingency or waste as theological problems, while some question whether death in itself is problematic. The suffering of creatures, human and non-human, is widely thought to be at the heart of the problem, though a few authors even question whether non-human suffering is a theological problem.

However, if *any* aspects of biological evolution can be associated with natural evil, then it seems that God is deeply implicated in that evil. Ever since the nineteenth century, when the question has been raised whether evolution is compatible with belief in a creator God, a standard Christian answer has been that God did not make things, but 'made them make themselves'.[6] In other words, God

---

[4]Holmes Rolston III, *Science and Religion: A Critical Survey* (Philadelphia, PA: Templeton Foundation Press, 2006), p. 134, quoted by Christopher Southgate, *The Groaning of Creation: God, Evolution, and the Problem of Evil* (Louisville, KY: Westminster John Knox, 2008), p. 2.

[5]For contrasting views, see Southgate, *The Groaning of Creation*, pp. 7–10; Henri Blocher, 'The Theology of the Fall and the Origins of Evil', in R. J. Berry and T. A. Noble (eds), *Darwin, Creation and the Fall* (Nottingham: Apollos, 2009), pp. 149–72.

[6]Charles Kingsley, *The Water-Babies: A Fairy Tale for a Land-Baby*, ed. Brian Alderson (Oxford: Oxford University Press, 2014 (1863)), pp. 146–7; Frederick Temple, *The Relations between Religion and Science: Eight Lectures Preached*

creates living things *through* the process of evolution. But this seems to imply that God either *willed* the violence, suffering and destruction of the evolutionary process (which calls God's goodness into question) or was unable to prevent them (which raises doubts about God's power).

Biological evolution, in short, seems to raise in a distinctive and sharp way the problem of evil: How (if at all) is it possible to speak of both the goodness and the power of God in the face of the evil we find in the world?

In terms of the classification outlined in Chapter 1, we can think of different approaches to this question as different types of dialogue between a scientific discipline (evolutionary biology) and a voice of the Christian tradition. What part does each voice play in shaping an answer to the theological question about God's goodness in the light of natural evil? As in Chapter 2, I shall first briefly discuss the extreme positions in my classification (types 1 and 5), then consider the middle positions (types 2, 3 and 4) in more detail.

3.2 Closing down the dialogue: Types 1 and 5

3.2.1 Type 1: Only the scientific voice contributes

Richard Dawkins begins one chapter of his book *River Out of Eden* with a famous remark by Charles Darwin to the botanist (and **evangelical** Christian) Asa Gray: 'I cannot persuade myself that a beneficent and **omnipotent** God would have designedly created the Ichneumonidae with the express intention of their feeding within the living bodies of Caterpillars.'[7] This leads Dawkins into a

---

before the University of Oxford in the Year 1884 (London: Macmillan, 1884), Lecture IV (n.p.). Online at http://anglicanhistory.org/england/ftemple/bampton/04.html (accessed 13 November 2017).

[7]Francis Darwin, ed., *The Life and Letters of Charles Darwin, Including an Autobiographical Chapter* (3 vols, London: John Murray 1887), vol. 2, p. 312;

reflection on the experience of purpose in nature. He uses a number of examples to argue that what natural selection maximizes is DNA survival.[8] (Dawkins's account reflects one particular position, of which he has been one of the most influential advocates, in the debate about levels of evolutionary selection: see Box 3.2.)

BOX 3.2: SOME CURRENT CONTRO-VERSIES IN EVOLUTIONARY THEORY

Levels of selection

Although evolution by natural selection has been a firmly established theory for many decades, there have been important debates among evolutionary theorists. One ongoing debate is about the level or levels at which natural selection operates.[9] Darwin, in his writings, sometimes describes it as operating between individuals, but sometimes seems to envisage *groups* being in competition, so that one group as a whole may be favoured over another by natural selection. From the 1960s to the 1990s most evolutionary theorists believed that any effect of natural selection favouring one *group* of organisms over another would be overwhelmed by the much greater effects of competition between individual members of each group. Some, such as Richard Dawkins, pushed this line of thought further to argue that the gene, rather that the individual, is the fundamental unit on which natural selection operates.[10] However, since the 1990s, some theorists have argued that under some conditions,

---

quoted by Richard Dawkins, *River Out of Eden: A Darwinian View of Life* (London: Phoenix, 1996), p. 111.

[8]Dawkins, *River Out of Eden*, p. 122. He uses the term 'God's Utility Function' to refer to what is maximized by natural selection. This does not of course suggest actual *belief* in a creator God: it is a rhetorical flourish, a metaphor used to dramatize his 'reverse engineering' approach to evolutionary thinking.

[9]See Elisabeth Lloyd, 'Units and Levels of Selection', in Edward N. Zalta (ed.), *The Stanford Encyclopedia of Philosophy* (Summer 2017 Edition), online at https://plato.stanford.edu/archives/sum2017/entries/selection-units/ (accessed 21 February 2019).

[10]Richard Dawkins, *The Selfish Gene* (Oxford: Oxford University Press, 1976).

group selection too can be a significant effect in evolution.[11] Therefore (they say) natural selection can operate at a number of different levels, including the group.

The Extended Evolutionary Synthesis (EES)

The standard neo-Darwinian view is that variation between individuals is caused by genetic differences, and natural selection operating on these genetic variations is by far the dominant cause of evolutionary change. In recent years some theorists have challenged this view, arguing for an 'extended evolutionary synthesis' (EES) in which other causes of evolutionary change must be recognized alongside genetic variation and natural selection.[12] These factors include the following:

- *Developmental bias*: the mechanisms by which individuals grow and develop from the embryonic stage onwards may place constraints on the forms and variations that can arise.

- *Plasticity*: individuals can change their forms in response to the environment. Advocates of the EES argue that in some cases the change of form may come first, and only later be stabilized by genetic changes.

- *Epigenetics*: chemical modifications to DNA molecules, which do not change the genetic information encoded by the DNA, play an important role in regulating the 'expression' of that genetic information and its effects on the organism. There is some evidence that epigenetic changes can be passed on from mothers to their offspring. EES advocates argue that this is another mechanism

[11]See David Sloan Wilson and Elliott Sober, 'Reintroducing Group Selection to the Human Behavioral Sciences', *Behavioral and Brain Sciences* 7, no. 4 (1994), pp. 585–654.
[12]Kevin Laland, Tobias Uller, Marc Feldman, Kim Sterelny, Gerd B. Müller, Armin Moczek, Eva Jablonka and John Odling-Smee, 'Does Evolutionary Theory Need a Rethink? Yes, Urgently', *Nature* 514 (2014), pp. 161–4; Kevin Laland, Tobias Uller, Marcus W. Feldman, Kim Sterelny, Gerd B. Müller, Armin Moczek, Eva Jablonka and John Odling-Smee, 'The Extended Evolutionary Synthesis: Its Structure, Assumptions, and Predictions', *Proceedings of the Royal Society B* 282 (2015), DOI: http://dx.doi.org/10.1098/rspb.2015.1019

of inheritance, alongside genetic inheritance, which is potentially important for evolution.

- *Niche construction*: in a simple picture of evolution, a particular combination of selection pressures in the environment form an evolutionary 'niche', to which organisms become adapted by natural selection. Niche construction theory emphasizes the active role that many organisms play in changing their environments (as when beavers construct their dams, for example). EES advocates argue that we should think of organisms actively constructing their evolutionary niches, not merely adapting to them.

However, the EES is controversial. Other evolutionary theorists argue that it overstates the evolutionary importance of factors like epigenetics, and that the effects described by supporters of the EES can easily be accommodated within a standard account of evolution by natural selection.[13]

Suffering is often a by-product of this process; for example, 'It is better for the genes of Darwin's ichneumon wasp that the caterpillar should be alive, and therefore fresh, when it is eaten, no matter what the cost in suffering. Genes don't care about suffering, because they don't care about anything.'[14] At the end of the chapter, his account jumps to human suffering, referring to the example of a disastrous road accident that claimed numerous schoolchildren's lives. He concludes:

if the universe were just electrons and selfish genes, meaningless tragedies like the crashing of this bus are exactly what we should expect, along with equally meaningless *good* fortune. ...

[13]Gregory A. Wray, Hopi E. Hoekstra, Douglas J. Futuyma, Richard E. Lenski, Trudy F. C. Mackay, Dolph Schluter and Joan E. Strassmann, 'Does Evolutionary Theory Need a Rethink? No, All Is Well', *Nature* 514 (2014), pp. 161, 163–4; Deborah Charlesworth, Nicholas H. Barton and Brian Charlesworth, 'The Sources of Adaptive Variation', *Proceedings of the Royal Society B* 284 (2017), DOI: http://dx.doi.org/10.1098/rspb.2016.2864.
[14]Dawkins, *River Out of Eden*, p. 153.

The universe we observe has precisely the properties we should expect if there is, at bottom, no design, no purpose, no evil and no good, nothing but blind, pitiless indifference.[15]

In other words, the phenomenon of evolutionary suffering is consistent with a materialist view of the universe in which the perspective of the Christian tradition has no place.

The bulk of Dawkins's discussion is concerned with scientific evidence and its interpretation. Then the conclusion just quoted makes a large leap from his scientific examples to a claim about the kinds of universe we should expect if there were, or were not, a God. The examples of evolutionary suffering in his discussion seem to be included mostly as rhetorical support for a materialist view of the universe reached on other grounds. Elsewhere it appears that those grounds are a reductive view of causation and causal explanation similar to that of Victor Stenger, discussed in Chapter 2 (Section 2.3.1). If science can give a causal explanation for the way the world is, there is no reason to think the world is God's creation. Richer and more complex views of causal explanation would call this conclusion into question (see Chapter 2, Box 2.3); Dawkins dismisses these, but does not offer much reason for doing so.[16]

In summary, Dawkins denies that the voice of the Christian tradition has anything to contribute to understanding evolutionary suffering. Only science, he thinks, has anything to contribute to this question, and what it offers is a materialist view of the universe in which there is no good or evil (and therefore no 'problem of evil'). Suffering simply occurs as an inevitable by-product of the evolutionary process. This view, though, is more asserted than argued for.

3.2.2 Type 5: Only the Christian tradition contributes

The clearest example of a type 5 response to the problem of natural evil and evolution can be found in young-earth creationism, which

---

[15]Ibid., p. 155.
[16]Ibid., pp. 112–14.

solves the problem by rejecting evolution. Young-earth creationists reject all the geological, biological and other scientific evidence that living things evolved by natural selection over billions of years. This scientific picture is replaced by an account based on a literal reading of Genesis 1–11, in which the universe is a few thousand years old, creation took six days and subsequently there was a cataclysmic worldwide flood.[17]

The problem of natural evil is sometimes cited as one reason for rejecting evolution. For example, Russell D. Moore has described how he was won over to young-earth creationism by watching a natural history documentary:

> Specifically, the problem for Christian theology is the picture of a python swallowing a pig. Is this what God created and called good?

> I find the primary text for understanding the age of the earth is Romans 8, in which the Apostle Paul reiterates the Genesis teaching that death and decay comes through sin. For Paul, this is not simply human bondage but the slavery of the entire created order.[18]

On this view, animal suffering and destruction are not willed by God, but result from the fall and human sin. In that case, the evolutionary account is a problem, because it suggests that there was animal suffering and destruction long before humans were on the scene. Therefore Moore rejects the evolutionary account. This response at least recognizes the seriousness of the problem of evolutionary evil, but then sidesteps the problem by rejecting the science that raises the issue. This refusal of any real engagement with the scientific voice is what marks out the creationist response as an example of type 5.

Young-earth creationism has well-known internal and external problems. Internally, attempts to read Genesis 1–11 as a single, coherent, literal historical narrative run into all kinds of difficulties

---

[17]E.g. Henry M. Morris, *Scientific Creationism*, 2nd ed. (Green Forest, AR: Master, 1985).
[18]Russell D. Moore, 'A Creationist Watches Animal Planet™', *Southern Seminary Magazine*, 74, no. 2 (2006), pp. 10–11.

and contradictions. Externally, it is more or less universally rejected by the scientific community. But quite apart from these difficulties, the young-earth creationist position may not actually help very much with the problem of evil raised by animal suffering, death and extinction. Moore's solution is that these phenomena are consequences of the fall, but other conservative scholars deny that this has much scriptural support.[19] Even if it does, troubling questions persist about the justice of a God who visits those consequences on animal species which presumably did nothing to deserve them. In short type 5, like type 1, seems an unpromising approach to this issue.

3.3 Revising Christian God-talk: Type 2

As we have seen, scientifically informed knowledge of the violence, suffering and destruction inherent in the evolutionary process seriously challenges Christian belief in an all-powerful, perfectly good Creator God. Those who feel the full force of that challenge but still wish to affirm faith in God may try to resolve the tension by radically revising Christian claims about God's power, goodness or both.

3.3.1 Rejecting a 'virile' God: Ruth Page

A revision of claims about God's *power* can be found in Ruth Page's book *God and the Web of Creation*, which she describes as 'an endeavour to keep belief, knowledge, experience and action together'.[20] Admittedly, there is some ambiguity about using this work as an example of type 2, because parts of Page's account are driven more by philosophical and theological argument than by explicit reference to science. As we shall see, however, it is clear that scientifically informed knowledge of evolutionary suffering and destruction is an important motivator for her account. Moreover, the radical and sustained way in which she follows through her

[19]For example, Blocher, 'The Theology of the Fall', pp. 165–6.
[20]Ruth Page, *God and the Web of Creation* (London: SCM Press, 1996), p. xix.

critique of traditional notions of divine power makes her book a particularly helpful example of this approach.[21]

Page forthrightly denies that God's creative work should be understood as 'making' or 'doing', drawing instead on two concepts found in the philosophy of Martin Heidegger: 'letting-be' and 'being-with'.[22] God creates the possibility for things to exist and for events to happen, but does nothing to determine *what* exists or happens. Alongside this 'letting possibility be', God 'companions' all things.

Although Page does not deny God's transcendence, her emphasis is very much on divine immanence. She coins the term 'pansyntheism' (as distinct from the more familiar **pantheism** and **panentheism**) to denote a God who is *with* all things.[23] This God 'knows and feels' what it means to be any kind of being, however simple or complex, and accompanies all beings in the unfolding of their possibilities. But God does not guide or direct natural processes such as evolution. Page writes of this as a 'constraint' on God, which prevents God from intervening to reduce the suffering caused by natural processes such as evolution. Humans, however, are under no such constraint, and have a moral responsibility to alleviate what they can of the suffering caused by natural evil.[24]

Where does this notion of God come from? Page makes clear that it is largely motivated by theodicy: 'I do not attribute any ... creativity [understood as making] to God because that inevitably leads to holding God responsible for natural evil.'[25] Elsewhere she puts the point more fully and forcefully:

I cannot imagine it possible to worship a God responsible for natural evil any more than one responsible for moral evil. ... To

---

[21]Others have explored these issues to some extent: see, for example, Arthur Peacocke, 'The Cost of New Life', in John Polkinghorne (ed.), *The Work of Love: Creation as Kenosis* (Grand Rapids, MI: Eerdmans, 2001), pp. 21–42. However, although this essay engages in a more sustained way with evolution, Peacocke's conclusions about divine power are more modest than Page's, and less clearly driven by the problem of evolutionary evil and suffering. Peacocke's response to that problem is more focused on the claim that God suffers 'in, with and under' the suffering of creation, a theme taken up by Christopher Southgate (Section 3.4).

[22]In German, *Gelassenheit* and *Mitsein* respectively: ibid., pp. 5–12, 42.

[23]Ibid., pp. 40–9.

[24]Ibid., p. 105

[25]Ibid., p. 165.

those who wish to affirm full-blooded ... [divine] making and doing, this version will appear anaemic. But the consequences of belief in a more virile God, who has to be responsible for the removal of around 98% of all species ever, but who fails to do anything in millions of cases of acute suffering in nature and humanity, are scarcely to be borne.[26]

This rejection of 'full-blooded' divine making and doing also calls for radical revision of other core doctrines, such as Christology and eschatology.[27] Eschatology becomes 'Teleology now!'[28] This occurs in any moment when the possibility of 'concurrence' with God is fulfilled by a human or non-human creature – for example, in human acts of love and freedom. Because God is eternal, God's 'involvement' in such moments makes them eternal: 'The fulfilments of God's purposes are not lost, but are, so to speak, harvested as the fruits of creation.'[29]

Page offers some acute criticism of ways in which God's creative activity has been conceived in the Christian tradition, and the damaging effects of those conceptions. Indeed, some of her targets, such as deism and William Paley's natural theology (see Chapter 4, Box 4.2), are widely recognized as inadequate ways for the Christian tradition to speak of God as Creator. Yet her own approach may also be theologically costly. For one thing, if God '[renounces] any use of power other than the attraction of relationship',[30] this seems to raise its own questions about God's goodness. To speak of God as *renouncing* power implies that God *could* use that power to overcome evil and bring about good, but has chosen not to. If so, it is not clear why this makes God any less responsible for natural evil, or why this view of God is any more 'to be borne' than the more 'virile' God whom Page rejects.

Also, it is not clear that Page is entirely consistent in her account of 'letting-be'. In the phrase just quoted, she suggests that God exercises 'the attraction of relationship'. However, elsewhere she

---

[26]Ibid., p. 104.
[27]Ibid., pp. 58–73.
[28]Ibid., p. 63.
[29]Ibid., p. 65.
[30]Ibid., p. 65.

rejects the view found in process theology (Chapter 2, Section 2.4.4), that God 'lures' reality towards certain outcomes. The problem with this view is that 'God in process thought has a preferred option', and if so, it seems to include the suffering and destruction of the evolutionary process – raising once again the question of God's goodness.[31] Yet her God also has a preferred option: creatures' actualization of love and freedom in each moment, in concurrence with God. If God exercises 'the attraction of relationship' to draw creatures towards that concurrence, surely God is still influencing the process, and the questions about God's responsibility for natural evil do not go away. On the other hand, if God really exercises *no* influence over how things turn out, how different is this account from Dawkins's view of a fundamentally meaningless universe in which good fortune and misfortune happen randomly?[32] Page might reply that there is a difference, because in her account, God 'harvests' the moments where concurrence occurs, making them 'eternal', while the moments where there is no concurrence 'come under judgement, and fall into eternal oblivion'.[33] However, if there is no eschatological hope apart from this – no assurance that God will bring about a time when good is fulfilled and evil overcome – then it is not clear what difference this harvesting and judgement of moments makes to the situation of God's creatures. In short, in her concern to protect God from responsibility for natural evil, has Page limited the possibility of divine action so severely that her God would hardly be missed?[34]

3.3.2 God as the 'ground of being': Wesley Wildman

An alternative response to the problem of evolutionary evil might deny or radically revise the claim that God is *good*. Wesley Wildman

---

[31]Ibid., pp. 47–8.
[32]Dawkins, *River Out of Eden*, p. 155.
[33]Page, *God and the Web of Creation*, p. 65.
[34]The phrase is borrowed from the philosopher W. R. Sorley, 'Surely a God that does not interfere will hardly be missed', *Moral Values and the Idea of God* (Cambridge: Cambridge University Press, 1919), p. 461. The original context of this remark was a critique of deism.

develops this response in a particularly vigorous way, through a broad-brush comparison between three types of theism.[35] The first is 'determinate-entity theism', in which ultimate reality is an all-powerful, perfectly good God who is active in nature and history. Second is process theism, in which God is not ultimate reality nor an all-powerful Creator, but 'one actual entity alongside many others, albeit one with a special role ... to maximize value in the cosmic process'.[36] Third is 'ground-of-being theism', which understands God as the ultimate reality, but *not* a personal God with humanly recognizable characteristics such as goodness.

Like many others, Wildman perceives a conflict between the claim that God is good and the nature of the cosmos as we understand it scientifically. He argues that ground-of-being theism outperforms the other two varieties in responding to this conflict. A standard response of determinate-entity theists is that this is the best of all *possible* worlds: even an all-powerful God could not create a better one. Wildman finds this claim scientifically implausible.[37] Also, the determinate-entity God is subject to the charge of negligence. A perfectly good God would far exceed human standards of goodness, such as parents' care for their children. But scientific evidence about the cosmos suggests that if it is created by a determinate-entity God, this God fails to protect creatures from harm and suffering, falling short even of ordinary human standards of care.[38] The God of process theism is not all-powerful, and is *unable* to protect creatures from harm. This God therefore avoids the charge of negligence, but (argues Wildman) does seem incompetent and therefore unworthy of worship.[39] By contrast, ground-of-being theism does not attribute personal qualities like

---

[35]Wesley J. Wildman, 'Incongruous Goodness, Perilous Beauty, Disconcerting Truth: Ultimate Reality and Suffering in Nature', in Nancey Murphy, Robert John Russell and William R. Stoeger (eds), *Physics and Cosmology: Scientific Perspectives on the Problem of Natural Evil* (Vatican City: Vatican Observatory/Berkeley, CA: Center for Theology and the Natural Sciences, 2007), pp. 267–94. See further Wesley J. Wildman, *In Our Own Image: Anthropomorphism, Apophaticism, and Ultimacy* (Oxford: Oxford University Press, 2017).
[36]Wildman, 'Incongruous Goodness', p. 272.
[37]Ibid., pp. 283–5.
[38]Ibid., pp. 277–8.
[39]Ibid., pp. 278–9.

goodness to God. God is the ground of *all* cosmic possibilities: the purposeless, violent and cruel as well as the creative, nurturing and just.[40] Therefore there is no gap between God's character and the character of the cosmos, and the tension dissolves.

Wildman offers some acute criticisms of common theological responses to suffering, and a perceptive account of the difficulties this issue presents to theologians. Yet his proposal, for all its wit and vigour, invites some critical comments and questions of its own.

First, he takes it as read that theology is a human construction, a futile yet captivating attempt to speak of what is ultimately unknowable. This means that any claims we make about God are inevitably projections from our own experience of human life and the world. For example, if we say that God is good, we can only understand what that means by analogy with human goodness. The challenge for theologians is to 'manage' such projection, avoiding its excesses and dangers.[41] This view informs Wildman's 'argument from neglect' against determinate-entity theism, outlined earlier.

Now, of course, reasoning by analogy from the created world to God is a time-honoured theological procedure.[42] It would, however, be regarded with suspicion by some theologians, who would insist that the analogy must work the other way around, as an 'analogy of faith' that begins with God's knowledge of us and God's self-disclosure to us.[43] But whatever side they take in that argument, many theologians would reject the view that theology is *only* a human construction. They would say that it must be an exercise of human reason *responding to divine revelation*. In relation to science, the task will then be to bring this reasoned response to revelation into constructive and critical engagement with scientific knowledge of the world. Those who understand theology in this way are less likely to think they are free to undertake the sort of radical revision Wildman proposes.

---

[40]Ibid., p. 282.

[41]Ibid., pp. 269–70.

[42]It is famously described by the mediaeval philosopher-theologian Thomas Aquinas (1225–74), in his *Summa Theologiae*, I.23.5, 6, online at http://www.newadvent.org/summa/1013.htm#article5 (accessed 7 February 2019).

[43]Cf. Barth, *Church Dogmatics*, vol. 1.1, pp. 240–1.

Second, as he himself acknowledges, Wildman's argument is based on broad types of theism. For the most part he does not deal with the particular features of specific faiths (except as examples in passing), let alone specific authors or theological positions. But this broad-brush approach can lead to over-generalizations and obscure the distinctive features of particular traditions. For example, he acknowledges that Christianity fits awkwardly into his framework because of its focus on the death and resurrection of Christ and its tradition of martyrdom: 'Christianity has always had an idiosyncratic approach to suffering because of its Christological lens.'[44] He suggests that this approach to suffering should actually make Christian theologians more receptive to his account of a God who is the ground of both good and evil. But this fails to do justice to the difference it makes if faith and theology *start* with the awkward, idiosyncratic story of Christ's incarnation, life, death and resurrection, rather than with generalized arguments about types of theism. If Christians start with that particular story, they commit themselves to faith in a sovereign God whose goodness and love are revealed in the person of Jesus Christ – whatever mysteries and puzzles this requires them to wrestle with.

Finally, we might ask what difference it makes whether or not we believe in the ground-of-being God. Even allowing that the universe needs a 'ground' of its being (which would be challenged by materialists like Richard Dawkins and Victor Stenger (Section 2.3.1)), what difference does it make whether we call that ground 'God'? Wildman indeed acknowledges that his ground-of-being theism is close to various other worldviews including some forms of atheism, and regards that as one of its virtues.[45] But this raises a question about its viability for Christian theologians. Wildman claims ground-of-being theism has a long history in many traditions including Christianity. He thinks the emphasis on a personal God is 'a post-Reformation distortion', which he hopes will prove to be a 'passing trend' in modern Protestantism.[46] Yet his approach requires us to abandon, or radically revise, much that is at the heart of the Christian tradition and is not peculiarly modern or Protestant, such

---

[44]Wildman, 'Incongruous Goodness', p. 293.
[45]Ibid., p. 282.
[46]Ibid., p. 269.

as Christology, **atonement**, resurrection, **pneumatology** and eschatology. For many Christian theologians, these theological costs will be too high to make this a viable approach to their engagement with the natural sciences.

Wildman's and (to some extent) Page's approaches bring to the surface some basic questions about the task of theology. To put it over-simply: if theology is essentially a construct of human reason reflecting on religious beliefs and practices, the radical revisions proposed in these kinds of type 2 dialogue may seem like attractive responses to scientific challenges. But as we shall see in the next section, theologians who understand their task differently will be less likely to think they are free to follow a path like Wildman's.

3.4 Christopher Southgate's 'only-way' theodicy: Type 3

According to Christopher Southgate, in the discussion of evolution and natural evil, 'robust science encounters theology at its most tentative. ... There is thus good reason for taking the main lines of the scientific conclusions with the utmost seriousness.'[47] Therefore, while he aims 'to give full weight to the Christian doctrinal tradition', he also wishes 'to learn from science about the way things really are'.[48] Such remarks locate his evolutionary theodicy firmly in type 3, where it represents one of the most influential and carefully worked-out contributions to the field. It is set out most fully in his book *The Groaning of Creation*,[49] and defended and further developed in a series of more recent publications.[50]

---

[47]Christopher Southgate, 'Cosmic Evolution and Evil', in Chad Meister and Paul K. Moser (eds), *The Cambridge Companion to the Problem of Evil* (Cambridge: Cambridge University Press, 2017), pp. 147–64 (p. 156).

[48]Christopher Southgate, 'God's Creation Wild and Violent, and our Care for Other Animals', *Perspectives in Science and Christian Faith* 67, no. 4 (2015), pp. 245–53 (p. 247).

[49]Southgate, *The Groaning of Creation*.

[50]These include Christopher Southgate, 'Re-reading Genesis, John and Job: A Christian Response to Darwinism', *Zygon* 46, no. 2 (2011), pp. 370–95; 'Divine Glory in a Darwinian World', *Zygon* 49, no. 4 (2014), pp. 784–807; 'Does God's Care Make Any Difference?': Theological Reflection on the Suffering of God's

In this as in many theological enquiries, how you ask the questions makes a difference to the answers you are likely to get, so it is worth noticing some aspects of the way Southgate frames the problem. He approaches it explicitly as a Christian theologian, and distances himself from the kind of philosophical theodicy intended to 'provide logical demonstrations of the goodness of God in the face of evil'.[51] His question is instead how Christian traditions of faith and practice should speak of the God whom they confess and worship. For these traditions, he thinks, it is the *ambiguity* of the natural world which poses particular questions. We find it easy to marvel at the rich variety of living beings and systems we see around us. Yet nature is also full of pain, suffering, death and destruction. Moreover, we know from evolutionary theory that these 'disvalues' are intrinsic to the process which generates life in all its richness and wonder.[52] The theological problem for Christians is that God is 'deeply implicated' in this ambiguity, 'through having created processes to which disvalues were intrinsic'.[53]

Southgate focuses on the impact of evolution on non-human animals, not to deny the seriousness of human suffering, but because Christian theology has too often ignored non-human creatures. He identifies two particular effects of the evolutionary process as 'disvalues' that require a theological response: the pain and suffering associated with the struggle for life, and species extinctions, which represent the complete loss of particular ways of being a creature in the world.[54]

How does Southgate address the problem he has framed in this way? He describes his approach as a 'compound theodicy' composed

---

Creatures', in E. M. Conradie, S. Bergmann, C. Deane-Drummond and D. Edwards (eds), *Christian Faith and the Earth: Current Paths and Emerging Horizons in Ecotheology* (London: Bloomsbury, 2014), pp. 97–114; 'God's Creation Wild and Violent'; 'Cosmic Evolution and Evil'.
[51]Southgate, 'Cosmic Evolution and Evil', p. 149.
[52]Southgate generally prefers the terms 'value' and 'disvalue' to 'good' and 'evil' in his discussions of evolutionary theodicy, perhaps to avoid begging the question about whether aspects of the evolutionary process *should* be considered evil. More recently, he has sometimes substituted the terms 'beauty' and 'ugliness', a move which goes along with a shift of focus from 'theodicy' to 'glory' as a way to make theological sense of an ambiguous world. See Southgate, 'Divine Glory'.
[53]Southgate, 'Divine Glory', p. 785.
[54]For example, Southgate, *The Groaning of Creation*, pp. 3–4, 9.

of various elements.[55] At its heart is the 'only way' argument: creation is under a constraint, such that an evolutionary process involving natural selection is the only, or at any rate best, way for creaturely life in all its 'beauty, diversity and sophistication' to come into being.[56] Even the sovereign God of Christian faith could not bring creaturely life into being in any way that involved less suffering and destruction. Crucially, this suggests that God *willed* an evolutionary process that entails suffering and destruction, because this must have represented the best balance between the 'good of realizing creaturely values and the concomitant pain'.[57]

This may be true at the level of species or the system as a whole, but the evolutionary process still has countless individual victims: creatures whose life mostly consists of suffering with little opportunity to realize their creaturely being. The theodicy therefore needs additional components. One is that God suffers 'in, with and under' the suffering of creatures;[58] the death and resurrection of Christ are the moment where this divine co-suffering is most intensely focused, and God begins the transformation of creation. This transformation will be completed in an eschatological future in which all the individual victims of evolution will be compensated by the ultimate fulfilment of their forms of life (Southgate borrows Jay McDaniel's term 'pelican heaven' for this argument). Finally, he argues that humans have a special calling to act as 'co-redeemers', cooperating with God for 'the healing of the evolutionary process'.[59]

Southgate's 'only way' argument is a version of what Wesley Wildman calls the '"best of all possible worlds" claim'.[60] Their differing attitudes to this claim are illuminating. Wildman believes the claim is needed in order to support the account of God's goodness that determinate-entity theism requires. He sees it as an essential defence against the charge that God is negligent. However, he thinks that in light of our scientific knowledge of the cosmos, we

---

[55]For a summary, see Southgate, *The Groaning of Creation*, pp. 15–17.
[56]Ibid., p. 48.
[57]Ibid.
[58]Ibid., p. 51 *et passim*, quoting Peacocke, for example in 'The Cost of New Life', p. 37.
[59]Southgate, *The Groaning of Creation*, p. 16.
[60]Wildman, 'Incongruous Goodness', pp. 283–5.

cannot assume this is the best of all possible worlds.[61] Therefore a key support for determinate-entity theism in the face of natural evil turns out to be very weak.

Unlike Wildman, Southgate considers the claim reasonable in light of what we know about cosmology and evolution.[62] Intriguingly, elsewhere he acknowledges that we cannot be sure of it, but 'must just reformulate [the "only way" argument] in terms of a *presumption* that a good and loving God would have created the best of all possible universes'.[63] The central argument in his theodicy, then, is not established independently as Wildman would wish. Rather, it follows from a prior belief in a good and loving God. Southgate defends this choice on the grounds of personal conviction and commitment to a Christian tradition of faith.[64]

This clearly sets Southgate's approach apart from Wildman's, which is a theoretical enquiry into concepts of ultimate reality '[using] suffering as a source of selective pressure on God ideas'.[65] Southgate's, by contrast, is an exercise in faith seeking understanding: 'an exploration, from within the confessing community, of the ways of God with the world, given a belief in divine sovereignty and divine love.'[66] To those taking Wildman's approach, Southgate's argument, that this must be the best of all possible universes, may look circular. But those who understand theology as 'faith seeking understanding' may regard Wildman's kind of theoretical enquiry as misdirected (even though Southgate praises Wildman's account for its honesty and incisiveness). If Wildman is a good example of a type 2 approach and Southgate of type 3, their disagreement lays bare some basic differences in the way the task of theology is understood and approached.[67]

---

[61]Ibid.

[62]Southgate, 'Cosmic Evolution and Evil', p. 157.

[63]Southgate, *The Groaning of Creation*, p. 48, emphasis added.

[64]Ibid., p. 22.

[65]Wildman, 'Incongruous Goodness', p. 268.

[66]Southgate, 'Cosmic Evolution and Evil', p. 149.

[67]Ruth Page's *God and the Web of Creation*, which I have also given as an example of type 2, is more ambivalent. Page acknowledges that she has been shaped by the narratives of a particular faith community (p. 124), and describes her book as 'an endeavour to keep belief, knowledge, experience and action together' (p. xix). It

Southgate's 'only way' argument has the basic structure of many theodicies: we can affirm the goodness of a God who has created a world with evils in it, because the goods of this world could not be realized without the evils, and the goods are worth the price. This line of thought has been criticized by various philosophers and theologians,[68] who argue among other things that by explaining and justifying the presence of evil in the world, mainstream theodicies can themselves become *sources* of evil. According to John Swinton, Christians should not be trying to explain or justify the presence of evil in the world, but to *resist* it by means of distinctive Christian practices such as lament, forgiveness, thoughtfulness and hospitality.[69] Southgate acknowledges the seriousness of such 'anti-theodicy' arguments. However, he thinks theodicy like his, done by people of faith seeking to understand God's ways with the world, can escape these criticisms.[70]

If Southgate's disagreement with Wildman highlights an important fault line between types 2 and 3, anti-theodicy criticisms of his 'only way' argument reveal a divide between types 3 and 4, which we shall explore in the next section.

3.5 Critically appropriating scientific insights: Type 4

3.5.1 'Mysterious fallenness': Neil Messer and Nicola Hoggard Creegan

In an earlier essay, partly motivated by the critiques of Christopher Southgate's type 3 approach discussed in Section 3.4, I proposed an

---

is probably fair to place her account closer to the boundary of types 2 and 3 than Wildman's.

[68]For example, D. Z. Phillips, *The Problem of Evil and the Problem of God* (London: SCM Press, 2005); John Swinton, *Raging with Compassion: Pastoral Responses to the Problem of Evil* (Grand Rapids: Eerdmans, 2007).
[69]Swinton, *Raging with Compassion*, chs. 4–8.
[70]Southgate, 'God's Creation Wild and Violent', pp. 247–8.

alternative approach to the problem of evolution and natural evil.[71] This approach begins with one of the central things the Christian tradition says about God's creation: that it is 'very good' (Gen. 1.31). The first chapter of Genesis fleshes out what might be meant by calling the creation 'very good': it portrays a world of peace and plenty, without predation, struggle, violence or destruction. So there seems to be a dissonance between God's good purposes for creation, as disclosed by biblical texts like Genesis 1, and the reality disclosed by evolutionary biology, which is marked by scarcity, violence and destruction.

Rather than resolving the dissonance by claiming that God willed such evolutionary disvalues, I argue that (in the words of Karl Barth) they '[do] not correspond with the true and original creative will of God'.[72] The fact that suffering and destruction are intrinsic to the evolutionary process in this world should be recognized as an aspect of evil, opposed to God's good purposes. If we try to explain how or why this should be, we will inevitably find ourselves facing a mystery. Informed by authors such as Swinton and D. Z. Phillips, I argue that focusing too much on questions of explanation can distort and misdirect our thinking.[73] Instead we should focus on what God has done to overcome evil through the life, death and resurrection of Jesus Christ, and on our response to what God has done and promised.

---

[71]Neil Messer, 'Natural Evil after Darwin', in Michael Northcott and R. J. Berry (eds), *Theology after Darwin* (Milton Keynes: Paternoster Press, 2009), pp. 139–54. The phrase 'mysterious fallenness' used in the section heading is a term coined by Christopher Southgate to describe Nicola Hoggard Creegan's, Celia Deane-Drummond's and my positions: Christopher Southgate, 'Response with a Select Bibliography', *Zygon* 53, no. 3 (2018), pp. 909–30 (p. 916). The following discussion focuses on Hoggard Creegan's and my accounts. Sadly, space does not permit detailed discussion of Deane-Drummond's rich and intriguing approach, which is focused on 'sophia', the divine and creaturely wisdom at work in creation, and associates evil and suffering with 'shadow sophia', the dark side of creaturely wisdom that comes under God's judgement through Christ's death on the cross. See Celia Deane-Drummond, *Christ and Evolution: Wonder and Wisdom* (Minneapolis, MN: Fortress Press/London: SCM, 2009), pp. 185–91; Celia Deane-Drummond, 'Perceiving Natural Evil through the Lens of Divine Glory? A Conversation with Christopher Southgate', *Zygon* 53, no. 3 (2018), pp. 792–807.
[72]Barth, *Church Dogmatics*, vol. 3.4, p. 353.
[73]Phillips, *The Problem of Evil and the Problem of God*; Swinton, *Raging with Compassion*.

One challenge facing this approach is that the evil is so closely tangled up with the good. As Southgate rightly emphasizes, the violence and destruction are an intrinsic part of the evolutionary process that has brought about the richness and diversity of life.[74] In *this* world, you cannot have one without the other, and this has been the case for all of the world's history that is open to scientific investigation. Yet that is not so different from many ways in which we experience this world as a tangled mix of good and evil. This is how I think we should understand the 'fall' story of Genesis 3. It should not be read as a history of our origins, but a mirror reflecting back to us the world as we actually inhabit it: good and beautiful, but also tragically flawed and broken.[75] The hope and good news in this perspective lie in the promise that it will not always be like this. Biblical passages such as Isa. 11.6-9 envision a future 'peaceable kingdom' promised by God, in which wolves live with lambs and lions eat straw like oxen. In other words, in this vision of a future world, there is no more predation, violence or struggle for existence. In the present world, that is almost impossible to imagine: a straw-eating lion would be a contradiction in terms. However, Christian readers find in these texts an eschatological hope made possible by God's reconciling and redeeming work in Christ. In that light, it should not be unimaginable that God can bring about a good future in which the 'lion-ness' of a lion and the 'antelope-ness' of an antelope are perfectly fulfilled without the need for killing and being killed.

Another question raised by this approach is how we conceptualize evil. If violence and destruction have been an intrinsic part of the world for all the history of the world that science can tell us about, my account might seem **dualistic**, representing evil as an independent cosmic force opposed to God. This would be a great mistake, which Christian theologians have usually taken great pains to avoid. My approach draws on Barth's creative reworking of a long-standing Christian answer to this puzzle. To avoid such cosmic dualism, a tradition of Christian thought going back to Augustine

---

[74]For example, Southgate, 'Divine Glory', pp. 784–5.
[75]My reasons for thinking that a historical fall of a first human couple is both implausible and unnecessary for Christian theology are explained in Messer, *Selfish Genes and Christian Ethics*, pp. 185–8.

of Hippo has denied that evil has any independent existence of its own; instead it should be thought of as a lack, or 'privation', of good (*privatio boni*).[76] Drawing on this tradition, Barth uses the term 'nothingness' (*das Nichtige*) to speak of evil.[77] By 'nothingness', he does not mean 'nothing'. Rather, he means what God rejected, or *did not will*, when God willed to create all things and declared them 'very good' (Gen. 1.31). As such, nothingness has a strange, paradoxical, negative kind of existence: it is the chaos, disorder or annihilation which threatens God's creation, to which God is implacably opposed, which has been decisively overcome through the work of Christ. My proposal is that some features of the evolutionary process reflect, not God's good creative purpose, but rather nothingness: the disorder and annihilation threatening the goodness of creation.

Nicola Hoggard Creegan offers an account similar in many ways to mine (though she also criticizes certain aspects of mine).[78] She rejects Southgate's 'only way' argument; she attributes evolutionary suffering and destruction to the presence of evil in the world, whose origin is ultimately a mystery. She makes creative and fruitful use of Jesus's parable of the wheat and the tares (Mt. 13.24-30). In the parable, a farmer sows wheat in a field, but his enemy then sows weeds ('tares', in some translations) in the same field. Rather than attempt to pull up the weeds and risk uprooting the wheat in the process, the farmer says, 'Let both of them grow together until the harvest; and at harvest time I will tell the reapers, Collect the weeds first and bind them in bundles to be burned, but gather the wheat into my barn' (v. 30). Hoggard Creegan uses this parable as a metaphor for the presence of good and evil throughout the cosmos. The good and evil are closely intertwined and continue to

---

[76] Augustine, *Enchiridion*, trans. Albert C. Outler, Library of Christian Classics, vol. 7 (London: SCM, 1955), ch. 4. Online at http://www.ccel.org/ccel/augustine/enchiridio n.chapter4.html (accessed 21 February 2019).

[77] Barth, *Church Dogmatics*, vol. 3.3, pp. 289–368. The remainder of this paragraph is taken with modifications from Messer, 'Natural Evil after Darwin', p. 149.

[78] Nicola Hoggard Creegan, *Animal Suffering and the Problem of Evil* (Oxford: Oxford University Press, 2013). See also her 'Theodicy: A Response to Christopher Southgate', *Zygon* 53, no. 3 (2018), pp. 808–20. One aspect of my account that she criticizes is my use of Barth's concept of evil as 'nothingness': *Animal Suffering*, p. 76.

grow together until the **eschaton**, when God will bring creation to fulfilment and will finally overcome evil.[79] As Southgate rightly comments, this account places Hoggard Creegan, along with Deane-Drummond and me, on the opposite side of a 'fault line' from him in terms of our *substantive* responses to the problem of evolutionary evil.[80]

When it comes to Hoggard Creegan's theological *method* or approach, though, the picture is slightly more ambiguous. Her account is deeply informed by scripture – for example, by recent scholarship on the portrayal of evil in biblical texts. She emphasizes that scientific knowledge must influence the way we read and interpret scripture: for example, a scientifically informed understanding of other animals will 'compel us to read the biblical text differently and to read theology with this new understanding of animals in focus'.[81] But this is entirely consistent with a type 4 approach.

What takes her closer to type 3 is the apologetic element in her argument. She aims to recapture what she calls a *divinitatis sensum* (sense of the divine) in nature. The evidence of God's hand in nature, she argues, is what will enable us to go on believing in God's goodness, even in the face of evolutionary evil.[82] In support of this aim, she surveys a number of recent developments and interpretations of evolutionary theory, including those described collectively as the 'Extended Evolutionary Synthesis' (EES; see Box 3.2). She argues that these reduce the importance of natural selection and competition as drivers of evolutionary change, and suggest a view of evolution more friendly to Christian belief than the standard account.[83] However, a critic might ask whether this gives a hostage to fortune. As we have seen (Box 3.2), the EES is controversial. If we depend too heavily on scientific developments to support theological positions, will we be tempted to be selective in

---

[79]Hoggard Creegan, *Animal Suffering*, pp. 127–37.

[80]Southgate, 'Re-reading Genesis, John and Job', p. 378.

[81]Hoggard Creegan, *Animal Suffering*, p. 23.

[82]Ibid., pp. 99–102. She makes this argument with reference to Job 38, in which God's answer to Job's complaint about his unjust suffering is to demonstrate the wonder and mystery of the creation, and the evidence it gives of the power of the Creator.

[83]Hoggard Creegan, *Animal Suffering*, pp. 110–26.

the developments we focus on, ignoring those that might challenge our theological conclusions? And what happens if scientific thinking develops in future in ways that are *less* friendly to the idea of a sense of the divine in nature? Will we then have to re-think or abandon that idea?

In short, Hoggard Creegan's account overall suggests a type 4 approach similar to my own. However, some aspects, particularly her appeal to new (and controversial) developments in evolutionary theory for evidence of God's hand in nature, lean towards type 3. To the extent that they do, they (like Southgate's approach) illustrate both the promise and the dangers of a type 3 approach.

3.5.2 Type 3 versus type 4: Southgate and Messer

According to Christopher Southgate, my approach to evolutionary theodicy 'does grave harm to the conversation between theology and the sciences'.[84] This, he thinks, is because it does not take seriously the way values and disvalues are interlinked in the evolutionary process. It therefore sidesteps the central problem that God is implicated in evolutionary suffering and destruction. It reflects an unwillingness 'to learn from the sciences about the way things really are',[85] and 'runs the risk of making theology appear too defensive, too bent on mystification, to be part of an authentic conversation'.[86] This critique brings to the surface some of the key differences between types 3 and 4. In particular, it foregrounds disagreements about what theology ought to learn from science, and what it ought *not* to learn.

In one sense, Southgate is correct that I am unwilling to learn from science about 'the way things really are'. What I mean is this: for Christian faith, the most fundamental thing to say about our world – the way things *most* really are, theologically speaking – is that it is God's creation. Creation is a theological, not scientific, category, so science cannot tell us whether or not the world is God's

[84]Southgate, 'Re-reading Genesis, John and Job', p. 384.
[85]Southgate, 'God's Creation Wild and Violent', p. 247.
[86]Southgate, 'Re-reading Genesis, John and Job', p. 384.

creation. Nor can science as such tell us what it *means* to call the world 'creation'. So if Christians want to know what it means to call the world 'creation', what can the natural sciences tell them, and what must they instead learn from the Scriptures and Christian tradition? More specifically, how should they resolve the dissonance I noted earlier, between the goodness of God's creation as depicted by texts like Genesis 1 and Isaiah 11 and the evolutionary view in which scarcity, violence and destruction are intrinsic to the generation of life?

In effect, Southgate resolves this dissonance by rethinking what we might mean by the 'goodness' of God's purposes. Knowing that suffering and destruction are intrinsic to the evolutionary process, he concludes that God must have willed such an evolutionary process. Perhaps this was because creation was under a constraint, so even an all-powerful God could not create complex life any other way;[87] in any event, the God who willed the end must have willed the means. This evolutionary insight then acts as a lens through which Southgate interprets the Scriptures. This leads him to give less weight to Isaiah's vision of the peaceable kingdom as an expression of God's good purposes. Instead he foregrounds texts like Job 38.39-41 and Psalm 104, which speak of God providing food for predators. He argues that such texts support the view that God's good purposes include predation.[88] In short, evolutionary findings can tell us something about how we should understand God's power, God's goodness and God's ways with the world.

I am more doubtful that finite and sinful human beings can gain knowledge of God and God's ways from our scientific investigations of the natural world. Guided by theologians like Karl Barth, I take the view that genuine knowledge of God and God's ways will depend on God's self-revelation. This does not mean, however, that theology has nothing to learn from the natural sciences. To borrow a phrase of Barth's, a science such as evolutionary biology can serve as 'an interesting commentary on a text which must first be known and read for itself if the commentary is to be intelligible and useful'.[89] Evolution can tell us plenty about the 'phenomena' (Barth's

---

[87]Ibid., p. 381.
[88]Ibid., p. 384.
[89]Barth, *Church Dogmatics*, vol. 3.2, p. 122.

word again) of the world we live in. But if we wish to understand what it means for this world to be God's creation, destined for ultimate fulfilment in God's good purposes, we shall need to read evolutionary biology through the lens of the Christian tradition, not *vice versa*. This basic theological commitment has informed the starting point and direction of my approach to evolutionary theodicy. In my account, as noted earlier, an understanding of God's good purposes is shaped by key biblical texts like Genesis 1 and Isaiah 11. The texts about predation that Southgate cites, such as Job 38 and Psalm 104, can be seen as signs that God provides for creatures, even in a 'fallen' world that does not yet fully conform to those good purposes.

Southgate thinks my approach is an evasion of the really hard problems of evolutionary theodicy. I, on the other hand, see it as re-framing questions that are often badly framed. I would ask whether Southgate is too ready to accept a problematic framing of these questions, which lends itself too easily to the kinds of radical revision proposed by Wildman that Southgate has tried hard to avoid.

3.5.3 The dangers of type 4: Henri Blocher on a historical fall

However, Southgate's critique does draw attention to one of the characteristic dangers of type 4 approaches: that they can drift towards type 5, effectively denying either the validity or the relevance of scientific insights. I do not think my account does this (though it is certainly a danger to be guarded against). However, it is possible that other type 4 accounts do. For example, Henri Blocher approaches the problem of evil as a conservative evangelical with a high view of the authority of Scripture, yet he wishes to avoid 'a **fideistic** approach, which totally severs theological concerns from scientific data'.[90] Unlike me, Blocher insists on interpreting Genesis 3 historically, so that the fall of a historical Adam was the origin of evil in the world. He denies, though, that phenomena like earthquakes, tsunamis, 'germs' or animal deaths were consequences

---

[90]Blocher, 'The Theology of the Fall', p. 150 (emphasis in original).

of Adam's fall, or for that matter a pre-human angelic fall. He attributes natural evil to humanity's damaged *relationship* with nature, resulting from Adam's fall. This view presents him with some challenges in accounting for evolutionary evils. In general he tries to meet these by denying that many phenomena we usually think of as natural evils really are evil, when viewed in theological perspective. However, this leads him into some scientifically implausible claims – for example, that pathogenic microorganisms would have done humans no harm before the fall. In order to account for animal suffering, he plays down its seriousness (failing to take account of scientific evidence of its intensity and the parallels between human and animal suffering),[91] as well as suggesting that our concern about it is largely a matter of inappropriate late-modern sentiment.[92] In short, Blocher sets out to develop a view that is faithful to Scripture and takes science seriously, critically appropriating scientific insights to a biblically formed view. However, he ends up being selective in the areas of science he engages with, and does not always succeed in taking scientific insights as seriously as they warrant.

3.6 Conclusion

The problem of natural evil is one of the toughest challenges that evolutionary biology poses to Christian faith. In this chapter I have reviewed a range of responses to that challenge, representing all five types of science–theology encounter in my classification. As well as closing down any dialogue between scientific and Christian voices, the examples I gave of types 1 and 5 (Richard Dawkins and young-earth creationism respectively) turned out to have major shortcomings of their own. They were therefore ruled out fairly swiftly as serious options.

The type 2 responses surveyed, from Ruth Page and Wesley Wildman, make radical revisions to the Christian doctrine of God in order to solve or circumvent the problem of evolutionary evil. I have suggested that for Christians trying to set up a dialogue

---

[91]On the scientific evidence about animal suffering, see Southgate, *The Groaning of Creation*, pp. 3–6.
[92]Blocher, 'The Theology of the Fall', pp. 166–8.

between scientific and Christian voices about God's goodness in the face of evolutionary evil, the theological cost of these approaches is too high.

The divide between types 2 and 3 (as represented by Wildman's and Christopher Southgate's approaches to natural evil) reflects basic differences about the tasks and methods of theology. By contrast, the examples I surveyed of types 3 and 4 showed greater agreement about the tasks of theology and the purpose of the science–theology dialogue. These examples reinforce one of my conclusions from Chapter 2: both these types give the voice of the Christian tradition a fuller and more satisfactory role than type 2 in shaping theological understanding in dialogue with science.

However, types 3 and 4 differ over the weight we should give to scientific voices in shaping a theological understanding of the world. Perhaps more importantly, the examples I have given disagree about the *kinds* of thing theology ought, and ought not, to learn from the sciences. These differences are reflected in the major divide between Southgate's 'only-way' theodicy and accounts like Nicola Hoggard Creegan's and mine, which attribute evolutionary suffering to the presence of evil in the world. For example, can scientific knowledge influence what we understand by God's goodness, as Southgate in effect suggests? Or as I would suggest, does this mean putting a question to a scientific discipline that it is not equipped to answer, in a way that may disrespect the integrity of science and distort the theological enterprise?[93]

In other words, the discussion of evolution and natural evil has highlighted what I see as some particular dangers and difficulties of type 3, which is why in my own account I have tried to develop a type 4 approach. I have to acknowledge, though, that type 4 approaches also have their dangers, as I suggested with reference to Blocher. Type 3 accounts may offer an important challenge and corrective to these. Therefore a second conclusion from Chapter 2 is also reinforced by this test case: while types 3 and 4 are viable

---

[93]Hoggard Creegan's apologetic use of new developments in evolutionary theory (*Animal Suffering*, pp. 110–26) suggests that she would, in a sense, be more willing than me to say that scientific knowledge can influence what we understand by God's goodness. As I suggested earlier, this is one respect in which her account is closer to type 3 than mine.

approaches to the encounter of theology with science, both have characteristic dangers, and each is well placed to check and correct the dangers of the other.

A final conclusion is worth noting, which was implicit in Chapter 2 but has become more evident in this chapter: substantive positions do not necessarily map neatly onto methodological approaches or types. For example, I have identified both Blocher's approach to evolutionary evil and my own as type 4. Yet I disagree with some of Blocher's key claims, for example, about whether the 'fall' of humanity was a historical event. My typology is concerned with methods and approaches to the encounter of theology with science. Each type in the classification may include different and even opposing accounts of the same substantive issues.

4

Evolutionary, cognitive and neuroscientific studies of religion

CHAPTER SUMMARY

The third and final test case of my typology raises the question of the relationship between science and theology in a particularly sharp way. This is the scientific study of religious belief, practice and experience. Three scientific approaches are considered:[1]

- The cognitive science of religion (CSR), which seeks to identify the cognitive mechanisms by which religious beliefs and practices arise and persist in human minds and cultures;

- Evolutionary accounts which explain religion either as an evolutionary adaptation in its own right or as a non-adaptive by-product of other adaptive features of human minds;

- Neuroscientific studies of religious belief, practice and experience, and theories about the neural mechanisms involved in such belief, practice and experience.

---

[1]An earlier version of some of the material in this chapter can be found in Messer, *Theological Neuroethics*, ch. 2.

Christian theology reflects on beliefs and practices which these scientific approaches seek to study and explain naturalistically, so what (if anything) should theology learn from these scientific studies? As in previous chapters, I survey answers corresponding to all five types in my classification (see Chapter 1, 'Chapter Summary'), beginning with the two extremes:

> *Type 1* includes sceptical challenges or debunking arguments against religious belief based on scientific explanations of religion. This leads into a discussion of *naturalism* (Box 4.2) in the scientific study of religion: these scientific studies may be *methodologically* naturalistic, but that does not in itself justify the *ontological* naturalism that the sceptical challenges promote.
>
> However, not all type 1 approaches are sceptical or anti-religious: I also discuss Justin Barrett's CSR-based 'universal natural theology' (Box 4.3), an attempt to argue in favour of religious belief on the basis of CSR evidence without appealing to scripture or other sources of divine revelation.
>
> *Type 5* could include the view that scientific and theological accounts of religious belief and experience represent separate domains of enquiry with nothing to contribute to each other. This may be a difficult position to maintain in this field, and I suggested in Chapter 2 (Section 2.3.2) that it is theologically unsatisfactory as a general policy. However, a historical perspective from Peter Harrison (see also Chapter 1, Section 1.4) suggests there could be particular cases where, in effect, type 5 is the best course to take.

Next, I consider the three middle positions in the classification.

> *Type 2*: a general example is Arthur Peacocke's radical proposal for reconstructing theology in the light of science. More specifically focused on the scientific study of religion is Eugene d'Aquili and Andrew Newberg's 'neurotheology'. I argue that Peacocke's approach is vulnerable to the sceptical challenges described under type 1, while neurotheology has significant problems as a theological approach.

Type 3 is represented by two examples. First, I briefly discuss a second type of natural theology proposed by Justin Barrett, 'confessional natural theology' (Box 4.3). Next is a more extensive account by Nancey Murphy. Drawing on the Catholic modernist theologian George Tyrrell, Murphy aims to show that CSR offers a good but incomplete account of religion, which can be complemented by a Christian account. However, I suggest that her reliance on Tyrrell means that this aim is not fully achieved. It also seems to limit the scope for the account to be shaped by the scriptures and the Christian tradition's reflection on them, meaning that the account may drift towards type 2.

Type 4: a model for this type is Karl Barth's engagement with Ludwig Feuerbach's critique of religion as a projection of human nature and values. Barth uses Feuerbach's argument to critique the kind of theology which begins with human experience. He argues that theology must *begin* with faith in God's self-revelation in Christ, in which case Feuerbach's sceptical question becomes irrelevant. I suggest that a similar theological engagement with scientific studies of religion can welcome the sceptical challenges surveyed in type 1, using them to critique (for example) Christian apologetics based on CSR or neuroscience. Scientific studies of religion could also have an ongoing critical and constructive role to play for this kind of theological approach.

As in previous chapters, I argue that types 3 and 4 both offer rich possibilities for theological engagement with these scientific fields, but both types have their own characteristic dangers. I consider type 2 more problematic, and its problems become particularly evident in relation to scientific studies of religion. The rejection of types 1 and 5 becomes less clear-cut in this chapter: examples of both these extreme types may have significant parts to play in the overall debate.

4.1 Introduction

The scientific study of religion raises the question of the relationship between science and theology in a particularly sharp way. The tasks of theology include articulating, in an intellectually rigorous and critical way, a Christian faith which has its roots in the Hebrew Bible and New Testament, and which has been formed over many centuries by traditions of reflection and practice in Christian faith communities. Christians generally understand their beliefs and practices to be, in some sense, a response to a divine revelation expressed ultimately in the person of Jesus Christ. They believe that in their worship, prayer, Bible reading and sacramental life, they encounter the God to whom their scriptures witness.

Those who study religion using the scientific approaches discussed in this chapter seek naturalistic, cause-and-effect explanations of religious beliefs and practices. These include the beliefs and practices of Christians who believe that they are responding to divine revelation and encountering the God who became flesh in Jesus Christ. So what are the implications of these scientific studies for theologians who reflect on the same beliefs and practices? Are they in conflict? Should theology be informed in some way by these scientific findings? Or are the scientific findings simply irrelevant to theological reflection on Christian faith and practice?

Before exploring possible answers to these questions, we must briefly survey the relevant scientific approaches, namely cognitive science, evolutionary and neuroscientific approaches to the study of religion.

4.1.1 The cognitive science of religion (CSR)

The central claim of CSR is that the way human minds work makes them naturally receptive to religious beliefs and practices. Moreover, our minds will naturally be more receptive to certain forms of belief and practice rather than others. Cognitive scientists of religion aim to identify the cognitive mechanisms by which religious beliefs and practices arise and persist in human minds and cultures.

One important idea in this field is 'domain-specific cognition'. The human mind is not a general-purpose reasoning device; instead, different forms of information are processed by the mind in specific ways. For example, faces are processed differently from other visual information. Domain-specific cognition is often linked to the idea that the mind is 'modular', consisting of numerous mental 'devices' with specific functions, though Justin Barrett (one of the founders of the field) denies that CSR is committed to a modular view of the mind.[2] CSR scholars often argue that some of these cognitive functions or devices interact in predictable ways to generate religion. For example, various authors refer to a 'standard model' in which beliefs about gods and other supernatural beings are generated by a *hypersensitive agency detection device* (HADD); these beliefs are *inference-rich* and informed by a *theory of mind*, and they persist because they are *minimally counter-intuitive (MCI)* (see Box 4.1). This kind of CSR explanation is often referred to as a 'by-product theory': religion is a by-product of cognitive processes that have other functions. This kind of view is typical of CSR. However, Barrett insists that the field is diverse, methodologically pluralist, and has 'no non-negotiable commitments' except the basic assumption that the natural characteristics of human minds can explain religious expression and the range of forms that it takes.[3] This insistence sounds a cautionary note, at least, about notions of a 'standard model' in CSR.

BOX 4.1: SOME COMPONENTS OF THE 'STANDARD MODEL' OF CSR[4]

1. *The hypersensitive agency detection device (HADD)*: a cognitive mechanism which tends to attribute unexpected events to the actions of *agents*. 'Hypersensitive' means that the device generates false positives more readily than false negatives: we are more likely to think an event was caused by an agent, when in

---

[2]Justin L. Barrett, 'Cognitive Science of Religion and Christian Faith: How May They Be Brought Together?' *Perspectives in Science and Christian Faith* 69, no. 1 (2017), pp. 3–12 (p. 7).

[3]Barrett, 'CSR and Christian Faith', p. 7; see also Justin L. Barrett, 'Cognitive Science of Religion: Looking Back, Looking Forward', *Journal for the Scientific Study of Religion* 50, no. 2 (2011), pp. 229–39.

[4]Michael J. Murray and Andrew Goldberg, 'Evolutionary Accounts of Religion: Explaining and Explaining Away', in Jeffrey Schloss and Michael J. Murray (eds), *The Believing Primate: Scientific, Philosophical, and Theological Reflections on the Origins of Religion* (Oxford: Oxford University Press, 2009), pp. 179–99 (pp. 183–9); Matthew Braddock, 'Debunking Arguments and the Cognitive Science of Religion', *Theology and Science* 14, no. 3 (2016), pp. 268–87 (pp. 268–9).

fact it was not, than vice versa. For example, if we hear a noise in our house, we may immediately assume it is caused by someone moving around, even if it later turns out not to be.

2. *Inference-rich concepts*: concepts associated in our minds with further characteristics, so that we readily draw inferences from the initial concept. For example, the concept of 'agent' is associated with many further characteristics that agents can be expected to have (they have intentions, preferences, etc.). Once we have identified a particular being as an agent, we very easily attribute these other characteristics to that being.

3. *Theory of mind*: we naturally think of other agents as having minds somewhat like ours, with thoughts, feelings, intentions and so on.

4. *Minimally counter-intuitive (MCI) concepts*: concepts that violate some, but not too many, of our normal expectations: for example, the concept of a human being who could pass through solid objects but otherwise resembled any other human would be MCI. There is good evidence that human minds tend to retain MCI concepts more readily than either fully intuitive or highly counter-intuitive concepts.

4.1.2 Evolutionary accounts of religion

Although CSR is distinct from evolutionary accounts, the two are fairly closely linked.[5] If humans have a combination of mental functions which interact to generate religious and supernatural beliefs, it is natural to ask how we came to have those functions. A frequent answer is that we have them because they were adaptive (they increased the chances of survival and reproduction) for our evolutionary ancestors. For example, it is easy to see how an agency detection device could have been adaptive for our ancestors, by

---

[5]Barrett, 'CSR: Looking Back, Looking Forward', p. 233.

enabling them to recognize potentially dangerous agents (such as predators that might attack them) quickly. It is also clear how a *hypersensitive* agency detection function could have been adaptive: mistaking a rock for a dangerous predator would be a less costly error than mistaking a predator for a rock. According to this kind of evolutionary explanation, religion is what Stephen Jay Gould called a **spandrel**: a non-adaptive by-product of other adaptive characteristics.[6] It is the mental functions such as the HADD that were adaptive for our ancestors; the tendency to have religious or supernatural beliefs was not adaptive itself, but arose as a by-product of those adaptive functions.

However, other theorists treat religion itself as an evolutionary adaptation. One of the best known of these is David Sloan Wilson, whose evolutionary theory of religion is linked to his defence of group selection as one of the levels of evolutionary selection (see Chapter 3, Box 3.2).[7] In a social species like ours, 'pro-social' behaviours like cooperation and altruism may be adaptive for the group as a whole, but costly for the individuals who perform them. For those behaviours to persist, the group will need mechanisms to enforce them and discourage 'free-riders': individuals who benefit from the pro-social behaviour of others without incurring any of its costs. Referring to examples such as the city of Geneva under the leadership of sixteenth-century Reformer John Calvin, Wilson argues that religion evolved as such a mechanism. Many Calvinist teachings, in his view, were norms for pro-social behaviour beneficial to the group as a whole. Calvin's teachings about God and God's relationship with humanity formed a 'fictional belief system', designed to motivate group members to conform to these behavioural norms.[8]

In Wilson's theory, religion is the product of biological group selection: religious beliefs and behaviours arise from genetically inherited characteristics, which have become so widespread in our

---

[6]Stephen J. Gould and Richard C. Lewontin, 'The Spandrels of San Marco and the Panglossian Paradigm: A Critique of the Adaptationist Programme', *Proceedings of the Royal Society B* 205 (1979), pp. 581–98.
[7]David Sloan Wilson, *Darwin's Cathedral: Evolution, Religion, and the Nature of Society* (Chicago, IL: University of Chicago Press, 2002).
[8]Ibid., pp. 98–105.

species because they are favoured by selection pressures operating at the level of groups. Others regard religion as the product of *cultural* rather than biological group selection: religious ideas, beliefs and behaviours are passed on through human culture, they change over time, and some persist and spread, by processes of cultural 'selection' analogous to the way natural selection works in biological evolution.[9] Some authors also argue that for a phenomenon as complex and diverse as religion, these various evolutionary theories need not be mutually exclusive: more than one could be true, with different theories accounting for different aspects of religion.[10]

4.1.3 Neuroscientific studies of religion

As the study of the human brain has advanced through the development of techniques such as functional magnetic resonance imaging (fMRI), interest in the neuroscience of religion has also grown. Some researchers have tried to identify areas of the brain involved in religious belief or experience. One early, and controversial, claim of this sort was that the temporal lobes played a major role in generating religious experience, and religious experience could be mimicked by stimulating them electromagnetically.[11] Other researchers have found that diverse areas of the brain are implicated in religious and mystical experiences.[12]

---

[9]Daniel Dennett, *Breaking the Spell: Religion as a Human Phenomenon* (New York: Viking, 2006).

[10]Jeffrey Schloss, 'Introduction: Evolutionary Theories of Religion. Science Unfettered or Naturalism Run Wild?' in Schloss and Murray (eds), *The Believing Primate*, pp. 1–25.

[11]See Michael A. Persinger, 'Religious and Mystical Experiences as Artifacts of Temporal Lobe Function: A General Hypothesis', *Perceptual and Motor Skills* 57 (1983), pp. 1255–62; L. S. St-Pierre and M. A. Persinger, 'Experimental Facilitation of the Sensed Presence Is Predicted by the Specific Patterns of the Applied Magnetic Fields, Not by Suggestibility: Re-analyses of 19 Experiments', *International Journal of Neuroscience* 116 (2006), pp. 1079–96; and for a critique, see Uffe Schjoedt, 'The Religious Brain: A General Introduction to the Experimental Neuroscience of Religion', *Method and Theory in the Study of Religion* 21 (2009), pp. 310–39 (pp. 330–2).

[12]For example, Mario Beauregard and Vincent Paquette, 'Neural Correlates of a Mystical Experience in Carmelite Nuns', *Neuroscience Letters* 405 (2006), pp.

Some neuroscientists have made proposals about the neurobiological mechanisms of religious belief or experience. In the 1990s, Eugene d'Aquili and Andrew Newberg developed a 'neurotheology' based on a complex neurobiological model of religious experience, which will be discussed later in the chapter.[13] More recently, Patrick McNamara has proposed a model of religious experience as self-transcendence, based on clinical case reports and brain imaging studies.[14] By contrast, Uffe Schjoedt is sceptical about such models, particularly if they make claims about brain systems or mechanisms specific to religion. He is also somewhat critical of approaches that focus exclusively on exceptional or extraordinary experiences. In his own research, he has concentrated on everyday experiences and practices such as prayer, and he has assumed (at least initially) that religious belief and experience are likely to involve the same neurobiological mechanisms as other aspects of human experience.[15]

4.1.4 Critiques

None of these approaches is uncontroversial. In relation to *CSR*, James Van Slyke has criticized by-product theories as causally **reductionist**, which (he argues) makes them both scientifically incomplete and philosophically problematic.[16] CSR is also accused of representing religion in oversimplified or caricatured ways, for example with its catch-all category of 'supernatural agents'.[17] *Evolutionary* explanations of religion, as we have seen, are

186–90; Mario Beauregard and Vincent Paquette, 'EEG Activity in Carmelite Nuns during a Mystical Experience', *Neuroscience Letters* 444 (2008), pp. 1–4.

[13]Eugene G. D'Aquili and Andrew Newberg, *The Mystical Mind: Probing the Biology of Religious Experience* (Minneapolis, MN: Fortress, 1999).

[14]Patrick McNamara, *The Neuroscience of Religious Experience* (Cambridge: Cambridge University Press, 2009).

[15]See Uffe Schjoedt, 'Does Praying Resemble Normal Interpersonal Interaction?' in D. Jason Slone and William W. McCorkle Jr. (eds), *The Cognitive Science of Religion: A Methodological Introduction to Key Empirical Studies* (London: Bloomsbury, 2019), pp. 203–10.

[16]James A. Van Slyke, 'Challenging the By-Product Theory of Religion in the Cognitive Science of Religion', *Theology and Science* 8, no. 2 (2010), pp. 163–80.

[17]For example, Deane-Drummond, *Christ and Evolution*, pp. 63–8.

diverse, and there does not seem to be broad agreement on which (if any) are correct. *Neuroscientific* approaches face conceptual, methodological and technical challenges affecting every stage from the conceptualization and design of experiments, through data collection and processing, to the analysis and interpretation of the results. These challenges do not make the neuroscientific study of religion impossible, but they increase the risk that studies will contain unsuspected flaws.[18]

However, to acknowledge problems, challenges and controversies with these scientific approaches is not the same as denying that they can make valid contributions to an understanding of religion. Assuming they can indeed supply valid results and insights, the questions stated at the beginning of the chapter remain: What bearing do these scientific studies have on the self-understanding of theology? What (if anything) should theologians be willing to learn from such studies, and what should they not be willing to learn? Once again, the typology used in previous chapters can help us sift through various possible answers.

4.2 Naturalism and neutrality: Types 1 and 5

4.2.1 Type 1: Only the scientific voice contributes – naturalism

In my first type of encounter between the voices of science and the Christian tradition, only the scientific voice makes any contribution to our understanding. In relation to the scientific study of religion, one form this type could take is the naturalistic view that the only true explanations of religious phenomena are natural explanations. On this view, claims that Christian faith and experience are a response to genuine divine revelation are false (or at best, irrelevant).

---

[18]Schjoedt, 'The Religious Brain'.

BOX 4.2: VARIETIES OF NATURALISM

'Naturalism' is an important term, but one whose precise meaning is not easy to pin down. According to David Papineau, for those who defined themselves as 'naturalists' in the first half of the twentieth century, it referred to the view that 'reality is exhausted by nature, containing nothing "supernatural", and that the scientific method should be used to investigate all areas of reality, including the "human spirit".'[19]

In the science and theology literature, a key distinction is often made between 'methodological' and 'ontological' naturalism. Again, these terms can be somewhat slippery, but can be roughly understood as follows:

- *Methodological naturalism* is about how the universe should be studied and explained scientifically. Andrew Torrance defines it as the view that 'the reality of the universe, as it can be accessed by empirical enquiry, is to be explained solely with recourse to natural phenomena'.[20]

- *Ontological naturalism* makes a claim about reality itself, not just how it should be studied: in Papineau's words, 'reality has no place for "supernatural" or other "spooky" kinds of entity'.[21]

It is generally assumed that science is, and should be, methodologically naturalistic. Many Christians support this view, arguing that the phenomena we observe and experience in the world *should* be explained in terms of natural cause and effect, not by invoking supernatural causes such as divine action.[22] They argue that religious believers and non-believers alike can practice science in this way with integrity, because methodological

---

[19]David Papineau, 'Naturalism', in Edward N. Zalta (ed.), *The Stanford Encyclopedia of Philosophy* (Winter 2016 Edition), n.p., online at https://plato.stanford.edu/arc hives/win2016/entries/naturalism/ (accessed 22 March 2019).
[20]Andrew B. Torrance, 'Should a Christian Accept Methodological Naturalism?' *Zygon* 52, no. 3 (2017), pp. 691–725 (p. 692).
[21]Papineau, 'Naturalism', n.p.
[22]For one example, see Kathryn Applegate, 'A Defense of Methodological Naturalism', *Perspectives on Science and Christian Faith* 65, no. 1 (2013), pp. 37–45.

naturalism does not make any claims about reality itself: it simply brackets out questions about the existence of God or a supernatural realm. There may even be theological reasons for being methodologically naturalist, because invoking divine action as a scientific explanation for natural phenomena not only closes down further scientific enquiry but risks turning God into a 'God of the gaps' and treating God as a cause among other causes in the material world (see 2.1 and Box 2.3). Methodological naturalism may be a safeguard against inadequate theology.[23]

However, some theologians have criticized methodological naturalism. For example, Andrew Torrance argues that it is not so easy to separate methodological and ontological naturalism as many Christians assume. He does not think Christian scientists should be methodological naturalists, because methodological naturalism involves assumptions about the world that are inconsistent with their Christian faith, and this causes a series of problems and dangers for Christians.[24] However, this does not mean Christian scientists should resort to supernatural explanations for natural phenomena. Torrance thinks they have theological reasons for adopting a 'humble' approach, which acknowledges that divine action is unlikely to be an appropriate scientific explanation. But they can do this without being committed to any kind of 'naturalism'.

John Perry and Sarah Lane Ritchie have defended methodological naturalism against Torrance's critique.[25] They argue that the debate about methodological naturalism is a 'red herring', based partly on a misunderstanding of the history of the term and debates about it. Paying attention to how scientists actually work – and in particular, how they handle anomalous results – suggests that methodological naturalism is not a matter of leaving God out of one's view of the world, but simply of different academic disciplines using the tools that are appropriate for those disciplines.

[23]See Messer, *Theological Neuroethics*, p. 28.
[24]Torrance, 'Should a Christian Accept Methodological Naturalism?', pp. 704–16; see also Alvin Plantinga, 'Games Scientists Play', in Schloss and Murray (eds), *The Believing Primate*, pp. 139–67.
[25]Perry and Lane Ritchie, 'Magnets, Magic, and Other Anomalies', pp. 1064–93. For Torrance's response, see Andrew B. Torrance, 'The Possibility of a Theology-Engaged Science: A Response to Perry and Ritchie', *Zygon* 53, no. 4 (2018), pp. 1094–105.

To discuss this view, we need to distinguish between *methodological* and *ontological* naturalism (see Box 4.2). The scientific approaches to the study of religion surveyed in the last section are methodologically naturalistic: they are attempts to explain the phenomena of religious belief, practice and experience in terms of natural cause and effect alone. However, the claim that only natural explanations are true goes beyond methodological to ontological naturalism. The scientific approaches themselves may not be ontologically naturalistic, but ontologically naturalist claims are quite common in the literature on the evolution, cognitive science and neuroscience of religion.

In some of this literature, an ontologically naturalist view seems to be a starting assumption rather than a conclusion drawn from the science. For example, it seems to function this way in David Sloan Wilson's evolutionary theory of religion: he treats religious belief as a useful fiction and offers an evolutionary account of how it proved useful in human evolutionary history. This attempt at naturalistic explanation may be partially successful,[26] but to the extent that it does succeed, it still does little to support the claim that religious belief *is* a fiction. In *Darwin's Cathedral*, Wilson more or less takes this claim for granted. Elsewhere, he does attempt what he calls a 'demolition job with respect to theism', arguing that religious beliefs have been shown to be empirically false by Darwinian evolution. However, his argument is unconvincing, appealing to an odd selection of examples for evidence and displaying a surprising lack of sophistication in his treatment of religious belief.[27]

Other authors think an ontologically naturalist view *follows* from scientific research on religion. They would generally not claim that scientific explanations of religion *prove* such a view. Paul Bloom, for example, recognizes that this claim would be fallacious:

[T]he question 'Why do people believe X?' is different from 'Is X true?' This is obvious when you consider other domains.

---

[26]See Messer, *Theological Neuroethics*, p. 21, for an argument that it is only *partially* successful.

[27]David Sloan Wilson, 'Evolutionary Social Constructivism: Narrowing (but Not Yet Bridging) the Gap', in Schloss and Murray (eds), *The Believing Primate*, pp. 319–38 (quotation at 338); for my critique, see further Messer, *Theological Neuroethics*, p. 29.

Psychologists who study why people believe there is intelligent life on Mars would be very confused if they thought their findings would bear on the debate over the actual existence of extraterrestrial life.[28]

However, Bloom and others think scientific explanations challenge the rationality of religious beliefs, by showing that the mechanisms generating the beliefs do not give rise to reliable knowledge.[29] This claim has been developed by others into more extended 'debunking arguments'. Matthew Braddock, for example, argues that we should suspend judgement about the reliability of the cognitive mechanisms that generate religious belief: we know that they generate many false beliefs, and therefore we are not justified in holding those beliefs in the absence of independent reasons for doing so.[30]

As Braddock makes clear, his debunking argument does not demonstrate that religious beliefs are irrational or false.[31] The status of his argument is akin to what Gregory Peterson has called a '**hermeneutic** of suspicion' supplied by evolutionary and CSR theories.[32] As we shall see, this will have a greater impact on some ways of setting up a science–theology encounter than others.

4.2.2 Type 1: Only the scientific voice contributes – universal natural theology

Interestingly, not all type 1 arguments about the evolution, cognitive science and neuroscience of religion are ontologically naturalistic or sceptical about religious belief. For example, Justin Barrett has proposed various ways in which CSR might relate to theology.[33] One of these is that it could indirectly support a 'universal natural

---

[28]Paul Bloom, 'Religious Belief as an Evolutionary Accident', in Schloss and Murray (eds), *The Believing Primate*, pp. 118–27 (125).

[29]Ibid., pp. 125–6.

[30]Braddock, 'Debunking Arguments and CSR'.

[31]Ibid., p. 268.

[32]Gregory R. Peterson, 'Are Evolutionary/Cognitive Theories of Religion Relevant for Philosophy of Religion?' *Zygon* 45, no. 3 (2010), pp. 545–57 (p. 550).

[33]Justin L. Barrett, *Cognitive Science, Religion, and Theology: From Human Minds to Divine Minds* (West Conshohocken, PA: Templeton Press, 2011), chs 8, 9.

theology' (see Box 4.3), which makes claims about God's existence and nature on the basis of reason and empirical evidence alone, without reference to Scripture or other sources of revelation.

BOX 4.3: NATURAL THEOLOGY

Justin Barrett identifies two forms of natural theology that he thinks are supported by CSR.

1. *Universal*: 'the attempt to use reason, self-evident truths, and evidence from the natural world to say something about gods or the transcendent, such as to demonstrate that God exists, and to demonstrate what properties God has.'[34] This is how natural theology is widely understood. It is very like the versions by William Paley and other eighteenth- and nineteenth-century natural theologians, who attempted to argue for God's existence or draw conclusions about God's attributes from evidence in the natural world.[35] By the early twentieth century this kind of natural theology had fallen into disrepute for various reasons.[36] In the 1930s, Karl Barth launched a powerful and influential attack on natural theology as an arrogant and futile human attempt to gain knowledge of God independently of God's self-disclosure to humanity.[37]

   However, various recent authors have attempted to revive different forms of natural theology, much

---

[34]Barrett, *Cognitive Science, Religion, and Theology*, p. 147.
[35]William Paley, *Natural Theology: Or, Evidences of the Existence and Attributes of the Deity* (London: J. Faulder, 1802).
[36]For contrasting accounts, see Alister E. McGrath, *A Fine-Tuned Universe: The Quest for God in Science and Theology* (Louisville, KY: Westminster John Knox, 2009), pp. 11–20; Matthew D. Eddy, 'Nineteenth-Century Natural Theology', in John Hedley Brooke, Russell Re Manning and Fraser Watts (eds), *The Oxford Handbook of Natural Theology* (Oxford: Oxford University Press, 2013), pp. 100–17.
[37]For example, Barth, *Church Dogmatics*, vol. 2.1, pp. 63–178.

more varied than the familiar Palcy-style version.[38] An
example is the second form described by Barrett:

2. *Confessional*: 'an attempt to augment, disambiguate and
    amplify theological claims of a given religious tradition
    by consideration of facts gleaned from the natural
    world, particularly the sciences.'[39] Barrett's source here is
    Alister McGrath, who has argued for a renewed natural
    theology very different from the eighteenth-century
    kind, which he severely criticizes.[40] McGrath's natural
    theology is not an attempt to 'prove' God's existence,
    but 'the enterprise of engaging and interpreting nature
    on the basis of the fundamental beliefs of the Christian
    tradition'.[41] He maintains that this avoids the faults of
    eighteenth- and nineteenth-century natural theologies,
    and is not subject to Barth's critique.

Barrett's CSR-based defence of universal natural theology involves
shifting the **burden of proof** in the evaluation of 'natural' religious
beliefs. Sceptical arguments based on CSR, such as Braddock's,
place the burden of proof on believers to show that religious
beliefs generated by natural cognitive processes are reliable. Barrett
draws on the eighteenth-century philosopher Thomas Reid and the
'reformed **epistemology**' of contemporary philosophers influenced
by him, such as Alvin Plantinga, to argue that the burden of proof
should be the other way round.[42] Beliefs automatically formed by

---

[38]The range of contributions to Brooke et al., *The Oxford Handbook of Natural
Theology*, gives an impression of this variety.
[39]Barrett, *Cognitive Science, Religion, and Theology*, p. 160.
[40]McGrath, *A Fine-Tuned Universe*, chs. 2, 3; see further Alister E. McGrath, *The
Open Secret: A New Vision for Natural Theology* (Oxford: Blackwell, 2008).
[41]McGrath, *A Fine-Tuned Universe*, p. 20.
[42]Barrett, *Cognitive Science, Religion, and Theology*, pp. 152–6. On Reid and
reformed epistemology, see Ryan Nichols and Gideon Yaffe, 'Thomas Reid',
in Edward N. Zalta (ed.), *The Stanford Encyclopedia of Philosophy* (Winter
2016 edition), online at https://plato.stanford.edu/archives/win2016/entries/rei
d/; Anthony Bolos and Kyle Scott, 'Reformed Epistemology', in James Fieser and
Bradley Dowden (eds), *Internet Encyclopedia of Philosophy* (n.d.), online at http://
www.iep.utm.edu/ref-epis/ (both accessed 1 March 2018).

our natural cognitive processes should be treated as trustworthy until they are shown to be otherwise. This move enables him to claim that CSR supports both cosmological and teleological arguments for the existence of God (see Box 4.4), since the reasoning that supports these arguments arises from natural intuitions about causality, order and purpose.[43]

BOX 4.4: ARGUMENTS FOR THE EXISTENCE OF GOD

Arguments for God's existence form a major topic within modern philosophy of religion. Various well-known ones are often described as 'classical' or 'traditional', and arguments resembling them can be found in mediaeval thinkers like Anselm of Canterbury and Thomas Aquinas – though it is not clear that these arguments had the same aims as their modern counterparts.[44] All come in many different forms, and have been the subject of extensive argument, discussion and refinement, as well as challenges and counterarguments claimed to refute them. The two most closely related to the science and theology field are:[45]

- Cosmological arguments: these generally maintain that the existence of the universe, or of contingent beings within the universe, requires the existence of a God-like being to explain it.

- Teleological (or design) arguments: these typically begin with some observable feature of the universe (e.g. the fact that it is ordered and intelligible, or that it is capable of generating life) and argue that this is best explained as the purpose of a God-like being.

---

[43]Barrett, *Cognitive Science, Religion, and Theology*, pp. 156–9.
[44]See Fergus Kerr, *After Aquinas: Versions of Thomism* (Oxford: Blackwell, 2002), pp. 52–72; Simon Oliver, 'What Can Theology Offer to Religious Studies?' in Maya Warrier and Simon Oliver (eds), *Theology and Religious Studies: An Exploration of Disciplinary Boundaries* (London: T & T Clark, 2008), pp. 15–29.
[45]For a survey of the various forms of these arguments and the main challenges to them, see Alexander R. Pruss and Richard M. Gale, 'Cosmological and Design Arguments', in William J. Wainwright (ed.), *The Oxford Handbook of Philosophy of Religion* (Oxford: Oxford University Press, 2005), pp. 116–37.

For Barrett's CSR-supported universal natural theology, appeals to Scripture or other sources of revelation are 'out-of-bounds'.[46] Insofar as a voice of the Christian tradition (as I have called it) responds to and reflects upon these sources of revelation, it has no contribution to make to this natural theology. *Taken on its own*, Barrett's universal natural theology therefore belongs in type 1. This certainly does not mean that Barrett's broader account of CSR and theology excludes the voice of the Christian tradition. Elsewhere he suggests various ways in which scientific and Christian voices could interact, one of which will be discussed later in this chapter. His universal natural theology could therefore be seen as part of a larger project which, taken as a whole, is not type 1. In earlier chapters I have suggested that type 1 approaches close down dialogue between the voices of science and the Christian tradition. It is clear from his overall account that Barrett does not want to close that dialogue down, even if the voice of the Christian tradition does not contribute to this particular aspect of it.

There is a clear apologetic purpose to Barrett's universal natural theology: to give rationally persuasive arguments for belief in God and respond to sceptical challenges. As we shall see in this chapter, such apologetic aims would be shared by many authors who reflect theologically on the scientific study of religion, though others would be much more suspicious of apologetic approaches. In any event, this apologetic argument of Barrett's depends heavily on a particular philosophical approach, a 'common sense epistemology' influenced by Reid. This makes it vulnerable to challenges which undermine Barrett's form of common sense epistemology, or argue that it does not apply to the religious phenomena he is discussing.[47]

4.2.3 Type 5: Only the Christian tradition contributes – neutrality and dialogues that should be avoided

One form that type 5 could take in this field is the view that scientific and theological accounts of religious belief and practice

---

[46]Barrett, *Cognitive Science, Religion, and Theology*, p. 147.
[47]For various challenges, see Bolos and Scott, 'Reformed Epistemology', section 7.

are simply different domains of enquiry: each is valid in its own terms, but they do not interact. This description might seem to fit the widespread view that scientific studies of religious belief are neutral with respect to the truth of the beliefs they study. If we want to understand religious beliefs, experiences or practices theologically, perhaps evolutionary, cognitive and neuroscientific accounts will simply be irrelevant, however interesting they are in their own right. Neutrality is suggested by the remark of Paul Bloom, quoted earlier, that 'the question "Why do people believe X?" is different from "Is X true?"'.[48] And even such a harsh critic as Daniel Dennett acknowledges that 'it could be true that God exists, that God is indeed the intelligent, conscious, loving creator of us all, and yet *still* religion itself ... is a perfectly natural phenomenon'.[49]

However, as Jeffrey Schloss observes, neutrality is not always what it seems.[50] For some authors it may reflect a genuine desire to avoid both pro- and anti-religious bias in the scientific study of religion. For others, though, it goes along with a generally sceptical stance towards religious beliefs, as in Paul Bloom's account. If such scepticism is held strongly enough, it will tend to deny that the voice of the Christian tradition has anything to contribute to the understanding of religious phenomena. This sort of 'neutrality' looks more like a type 1 than a type 5 position. In Pascal Boyer's words, 'people who think that we have religion because religion is *true* ... will find little in this book [*Religion Explained*] to support their views.'[51]

All this suggests that in relation to scientific studies of religion, this version of type 5 might be a difficult position to sustain. I also suggested in Chapter 2 that there are theological reasons for being uneasy with it as a general policy. Could there, however, be particular *areas* of science that theology is better not engaging with; and if so, are evolutionary, cognitive and neuroscientific studies of religion among them?

One possible reason for thinking this is suggested by an observation from the historian Peter Harrison: the very idea that

---

[48]Bloom, 'Religious Belief as an Evolutionary Accident', p. 125.
[49]Dennett, *Breaking the Spell*, p. 25.
[50]Schloss, 'Introduction', pp. 10–12.
[51]Pascal Boyer, *Religion Explained: The Evolutionary Origins of Religious Thought* (New York: Basic Books, 2001), p. 48.

there is something called 'religion', which can be studied and explained 'scientifically', reflects major shifts between the middle ages and modernity in the ways both 'science' and 'religion' are understood.[52] To mediaeval scholars, the idea that there could be a 'science' that studies 'religion' would have been unintelligible, because for them, 'science' and 'religion' (or more accurately, their Latin equivalents *scientia* and *religio*) referred to virtues or qualities of character (see Section 1.4). Harrison is simply making a historical point, but if he is right, this could raise the question whether a dialogue between these scientific voices and the voice of the Christian tradition is even possible. Evolutionary, cognitive and neuroscientific approaches study Christian faith and practice as a 'religion' in the modern sense. If Christians' understanding of their faith and practice is profoundly shaped by the Scriptures and a tradition that extends back through ancient and mediaeval times, scientific and Christian perspectives on 'Christianity' might be so different that they were irrelevant to one another, and a dialogue between scientific and Christian voices would obscure, not promote, understanding.[53]

There could of course be good reasons not to draw this stark conclusion. For example, the Christian tradition has a modern as well as ancient and mediaeval history, and this might create enough common ground between Christian self-understanding and the scientific perspectives to allow a fruitful dialogue. Many science and theology authors do think that the dialogue is possible and worth having, as we shall see throughout this chapter. However, Harrison's point is at least a reminder that we shall need to set this dialogue up very carefully to avoid distorted and misleading conclusions. And it does draw attention to the possibility that there could in principle be certain dialogues that are better not attempted, at least while the relevant scientific discourses take their present forms.

---

[52]Harrison, *The Territories of Science and Religion*, pp. 83–4.
[53]A similar point is made about CSR and 'neurotheology' (see Section 4.3.2) by Markus Mühling, *Resonances: Neurobiology, Evolution and Theology. Evolutionary Niche Construction, the Ecological Brain and Relational-Narrative Theology* (Göttingen: Vandenhoeck & Ruprecht, 2014), pp. 92–7, 222. Mühling is committed to theological dialogue with neuroscience more generally, but is highly critical of these particular approaches and doubtful of their relevance to Christian theology.

4.3 Reconstructing theology: Type 2

4.3.1 Arthur Peacocke: Seeking Christian credibility

Arthur Peacocke was one of the acknowledged leaders of the science and theology field in the later twentieth century. In the title of one of his books, his intellectual project is described as a 'quest for Christian credibility' in a scientific age.[54] For Peacocke this quest includes an apologetic strategy that attaches great importance to scientific findings.[55] He adopts a method of 'inference to the best explanation' (IBE), and maintains that a diverse range of data about the world, taken together, are best explained by the existence of 'an *Ultimate Reality, God*'.[56] While not an area with which Peacocke engages in depth, religious experiences are one component of this picture: they can be understood as natural phenomena, 'mediated by the constituents of the world', but also as ways in which God uses those 'constituents of the world' to communicate with human beings.[57]

Peacocke's 'quest for Christian credibility' involves not only an apologetic strategy but a radical agenda for reconstructing theology. He is impressed by the high status of the natural sciences and the poor reputation of theology in the academic world. To recover its intellectual status, he believes, theology must be radically revised in both method and content. Theology should stop appealing to the authority of Bible, church and tradition, and should adopt methods more like the natural sciences.[58] Peacocke has a high view of the place theology ought to occupy in human knowledge. In several publications he sets out a hierarchy of the sciences in order of increasing complexity. Theology occupies the top place because,

---

[54]Arthur Peacocke, *God and Science: A Quest for Christian Credibility* (London: SCM Press, 1996).

[55]See the comments on type 2 in Chapter 1, Section 1.5, for more on what 'apologetics' means in Peacocke's case.

[56]Arthur Peacocke, *Paths from Science towards God: The End of All Our Exploring* (Oxford: Oneworld, 2001), pp. 129–30, emphasis in original.

[57]Ibid., pp. 120–5, 130 (quotation at p. 121).

[58]E.g. Peacocke, *Paths from Science towards God*, pp. 18–36.

in James Van Slyke's words, 'it integrates all of the other levels of explanation into a transcendent reality that is able to go beyond the history of the universe itself'.[59] But the theology which occupies this place must be shaped to a large extent by natural scientific voices, and it is clear that what I have called the voice of the Christian tradition must be adjusted wherever necessary to conform to a scientific view of the world.[60]

Peacocke's apologetic strategy and agenda for reconstructing theology offer a clear (and very influential) example of type 2. As already noted, the phenomena of religious experience play some part (though not a major one) in his account. The literature more specifically focused on the scientific study of religious belief, experience and practice includes further examples of type 2 interactions.

4.3.2 Neurotheology

One is the 'neurotheology' first developed by Eugene d'Aquili and Andrew Newberg in the 1990s. In its original form, this includes a neurobiological model in which religious beliefs and experiences are generated by the functioning and interaction of various 'cognitive operators' in the brain. For example, a 'causal operator', which enables us to perceive cause and effect, may generate ideas of gods, while a 'holistic operator' may generate the mystical experience of 'absolute unitary being', in which we lose all sense of the passage of time and the difference between self and other.[61] These cognitive functions meet needs that have been hardwired into our brains by evolution, so 'religions and God won't go away'.[62] D'Aquili and Newberg emphasize that this is not an attempt to *reduce* religious and mystical experience to nothing more than the product of brain activity. They argue that everyday experience is mediated by similar

---

[59]Van Slyke, 'Challenging the By-Product Theory', p. 175.
[60]For a similar assessment of Peacocke, see Polkinghorne, *Science and the Trinity*, pp. 20–6.
[61]Eugene G. d'Aquili and Andrew B. Newberg, 'The Neuropsychological Basis of Religions, or Why God Won't Go Away', *Zygon* 33, no. 2 (1998), pp. 187–201.
[62]Ibid., p. 198.

mechanisms, and religious and mystical experience has just as strong a claim to be regarded as genuinely real.[63]

D'Aquili and Newberg also think their model can reshape the methods and content of theology. They propose that by understanding the neurobiological mechanisms of religious belief, it will be possible to construct a 'metatheology': that is, 'the general principles describing and, implicitly, the rules for constructing any concrete theological system'.[64] They also claim that neuroscientific studies can generate a 'megatheology': a theological system with such universal characteristics that most or all major religions could adopt it, which might even generate a new theology more universal in scope than current theologies.[65] Since the metatheology and megatheology are generated principally by neuroscience, these claims place d'Aquili and Newberg's neurotheology close to the borderline between types 1 and 2 in my classification. Their account does suggest *some* engagement with the voices of religious (including Christian) traditions, so it is probably best placed in type 2.

Newberg's more recent book *Principles of Neurotheology* differs in various ways from his earlier co-authored works.[66] He is more cautious about proposing specific mechanisms for religious experience, and avoids the language of 'causal operators', though he does still envisage specific cognitive *processes* associated with different parts of the brain.[67] He is also more ambivalent about the relationship of different voices in the science–theology encounter. For example, he writes that neuroscientific and theological perspectives 'should have similar, and reciprocal, emphasis in the overall dialogue between neuroscience and theology',[68] which might suggest a type 3 relationship.

However, the book as a whole does not really deliver on that aim. Newberg continues to advocate a metatheology and megatheology

---

[63]Ibid., pp. 198–201.
[64]D'Aquili and Newberg, *The Mystical Mind*, p. 195.
[65]Ibid., p. 198.
[66]Andrew B. Newberg, *Principles of Neurotheology* (Farnham: Ashgate, 2010); Eugene d'Aquili died in 1998, not long before the publication of *The Mystical Mind*.
[67]Newberg, *Principles of Neurotheology*, pp. 73–7.
[68]Ibid., p. 54.

shaped principally by neuroscience.[69] He also proposes a 'neurotheological hermeneutic' in which an understanding of the brain's functioning governs the way theological and philosophical concepts and religious experiences are interpreted.[70] Even in a chapter entitled 'Reflections on Major Topics of Theology',[71] most of the discussion is focused on how brain processes and mechanisms might be operating when we struggle to understand theological doctrines, or how the brain might make it possible for us to go through a series of steps leading to salvation. The voice of the Christian tradition, and the voices of theologians reflecting in depth on it, are more rarely heard. In general, one gets a clear sense of the neuroscientific questions that Newberg thinks are worth asking about religious belief and practice, but much less sense of what the theological questions look like or how they may be investigated. Overall, Newberg's view of the relationship between scientific and Christian voices still seems best described by my type 2.[72]

Type 2 approaches do allow for genuine dialogue between scientific and Christian voices in shaping theological understanding, but the dominance of the scientific voices can lead to problems with the resulting theological account. One is that it may focus too much on aspects of belief, experience and practice that are relatively unimportant to a particular faith tradition, and neglect aspects which that tradition regards as more central. For example, neurotheology has been criticized for focusing so much on extraordinary mystical and religious experiences, which in some Christian theological traditions would not be seen as central and might indeed be regarded with suspicion.[73]

A related problem concerns Newberg's claim that there is a common core to mystical and religious experience across many

---

[69]Ibid., pp. 64–6.
[70]Ibid., pp. 88–114.
[71]Ibid., pp. 221–47.
[72]Newberg aims to engage with a wide range of religious traditions, but in keeping with the focus of this book, I have only considered the implications of his work for *Christian* theology.
[73]Mühling, *Resonances*, pp. 92–7, 222; Wolfgang Achtner and Ulrich Ott, 'Protestantism and Mysticism from the Perspective of Neuroscience', *Theology and Science* 11, no. 3 (2013), pp. 208–23.

faiths, which could be explained neuroscientifically and used as the basis for a metatheology and megatheology. It has indeed often been thought that there is such a common core, but this has been strongly challenged (for example) by Steven T. Katz.[74] More generally, the idea of a metatheology makes some very questionable assumptions about how theology actually works. If theology is (as many theologians would say) the rigorous working-out of a particular faith tradition and its implications, the search for a 'metatheology' supposed to be applicable to many different traditions may fail to respect the distinctive and particular character of those different traditions.[75]

It is clear how such problems can arise from a type 2 approach to this field in particular, in which researchers aim to understand natural mechanisms that shape religious thinking, experience and practice. If a scientific discipline plays the dominant role in shaping theological understanding, it will be easy for the resulting account of theology to emphasize aspects that most lend themselves to being studied and theorized scientifically. This may mean that central features of Christian faith and practice, and some of Christian theology's most characteristic methods and content, are neglected or sidelined, as Markus Mühling complains.[76] It is easy to see how the experience of absolute unitary being might attract more neuroscientific attention than the practices of saying grace before meals or helping a fellow believer in distress (to use two of Mühling's examples), but a neurotheology centred on such extraordinary experiences may not in the end be recognizable to many Christian theologians or Christian believers.

This may not be such a concern for theologians such as Arthur Peacocke, who believe that the content and methods of Christian theology must change radically to be credible in a scientific age. If

---

[74]Steven T. Katz, 'General Editor's Introduction', in Steven T. Katz (ed.), *Comparative Mysticism: An Anthology of Original Sources* (Oxford: Oxford University Press, 2013), pp. 3–22.

[75]The emphasis on the particularity of theological traditions is especially, though not only, associated with **postliberal** theology. For contrasting assessments of postliberalism, see DeHart, *The Trial of the Witnesses*; John Wright (ed.), *Postliberal Theology and the Church Catholic: Conversations with George Lindbeck, David Burrell, and Stanley Hauerwas* (Grand Rapids, MI: Baker Academic, 2012).

[76]Mühling, *Resonances*, p. 97.

Peacocke is right, Newberg's neurotheology may seem an attractive way forward. However, scientific studies of religion may challenge Peacocke's own apologetic strategy and theological approach. Recall that Peacocke uses a method of IBE to argue that 'all-that-is and all-that-is-becoming' is best explained by the existence of God. CSR offers a naturalistic account of how humans might be predisposed to believe in such a God and to interpret natural phenomena in a way that supports their belief. This naturalistic account informs the debunking arguments of authors like Bloom and Braddock, that the rational status of religious belief is dubious because the cognitive processes giving rise to it are unreliable (see Section 4.2.2). Such debunking arguments cast suspicion on Peacocke's argument: if we are attracted by his conclusion that God is the best explanation of 'all-that-is', this may have more to do with our cognitive biases than the strength of his argument. This objection does not defeat Peacocke's argument outright, but does challenge and weaken it.[77] A type 2 approach like Peacocke's, which relies so heavily on interpreting scientific data in a certain way to make the case for belief in God, is more vulnerable to this kind of scientific hermeneutic of suspicion (as Gregory Peterson calls it) than some of the other approaches I shall discuss under types 3 and 4.

4.4 Correlating science and Christian tradition: Type 3

The literature on the evolution, cognitive science and neuroscience of religion includes various examples of my third type of approach: accounts in which the voices of science and the Christian tradition both contribute to theological understanding, but neither dominates. In this section I shall discuss two examples.

---

[77]Justin Barrett, in his CSR-based 'universal natural theology', in effect tries to counter this objection by shifting the burden of proof in these arguments onto the sceptics: *Cognitive Science, Religion, and Theology*, pp. 152–6. As I noted earlier, however, his argument for shifting the burden of proof is itself open to various kinds of challenge (see Section 4.2.2).

4.4.1 Justin Barrett's confessional natural theology

One brief account is Justin Barrett's proposal for how CSR may contribute to 'confessional natural theology' (see Box 4.3).[78] He suggests various possible contributions of CSR. For example, its account of the human propensity to believe in gods might support the claim in Calvinist theology that humans have an innate *sensus divinitatis*, or sense of the divine. Moreover, Barrett thinks, CSR might help to settle the differences between competing accounts of this sense of the divine.[79] Other areas to which CSR may contribute include 'explaining patterns of theological development in the past ... and predicting where theological thought might be going in the future',[80] understanding the way communication takes place through Scriptures and religious teaching, and informing the decisions made by religious leaders about such things as the conduct of worship.[81]

Barrett claims that '[t]he theologian who fails to appreciate the contributions of cognitive science will rapidly find himself or herself trafficking in outmoded ways of thinking and unable to connect with the concerns of contemporary audiences'.[82] However, is not clear how significant the contributions from CSR really are in some of his examples. For instance, he suggests 'relevance theory' predicts that scriptures will have higher relevance than other texts for believers, who will therefore invest more cognitive resources in reading and understanding even difficult scriptural texts. This may well be so, but it is unclear how much this finding adds to

---

[78]Some versions of confessional natural theology might be better described as type 4 approaches than type 3: McGrath's version might fit in this category, since he describes it as 'a subordinate aspect of revealed theology' (*A Fine-Tuned Universe*, p. 20). However, in Barrett's hands, the scientific voice plays a large enough role that his account is best located in type 3.

[79]Barrett, *Cognitive Science, Religion, and Theology*, pp. 161–2; see John Calvin, *Institutes of the Christian Religion*, trans. Henry Beveridge (Grand Rapids, MI: Eerdmans, n.d.), book 1, ch. 3.

[80]Barrett, *Cognitive Science, Religion, and Theology*, p. 163.

[81]Ibid., pp. 163–7.

[82]Ibid., p. 168.

a theological account of scripture and its place in the Church.[83] However, as Barrett acknowledges, the study of these interactions is only just beginning, so perhaps a more intensive dialogue between CSR scholars and theologians may generate more significant findings in future.

4.4.2 Nancey Murphy, George Tyrrell and CSR

A fuller account of how CSR might interact with theology is offered by Nancey Murphy.[84] She reads Pascal Boyer's account of CSR alongside a theory of the development of religion developed by the Catholic modernist theologian George Tyrrell at the turn of the twentieth century. For Tyrrell, divine revelation is primarily an inward spiritual experience, and secondarily 'the record or expression by which that experience is retained and communicated to others'.[85] Such expressions of the experience of revelation are found in scripture and in Christian dogmas; they are 'prophetic' expressions of revelation using symbolic, imaginative and metaphorical language. Theology is a second-order reflection on these expressions of revelation, an attempt to systematize them and integrate them with other aspects of culture, including science.[86]

Murphy argues that Boyer's account of CSR can easily be integrated with Tyrrell's model: 'Tyrrell shared with contemporary cognitive science of religion the understanding of religion as a natural phenomenon, developing in history according to "natural laws of religious psychology".'[87] These 'natural laws' are supplied by CSR. But for Tyrrell, the life of faith and morality is shaped by the spiritual

---

[83]For example, Angus Paddison, *Scripture: A Very Theological Proposal* (London: T & T Clark, 2009).

[84]Nancey Murphy, 'Cognitive Science and the Evolution of Religion: A Philosophical and Theological Appraisal', in Schloss and Murray, *The Believing Primate*, pp. 265–77.

[85]George Tyrrell, *Through Scylla and Charibdis: Or the Old Theology and the New* (London: Longmans, Green and Co., 1907), p. 268, quoted by Ma. Delia A. Candelario, 'George Tyrrell and Karl Rahner: A Dialogue on Revelation', *Heythrop Journal* 50 (2009), pp. 44–57 (p. 45).

[86]Murphy, 'Cognitive Science and the Evolution of Religion', p. 272.

[87]Ibid., p. 273.

impulses 'given from above'.[88] Therefore, Murphy argues, theology must go beyond CSR to give an account of how divine action shapes the development of thought and practice described by the latter. She is well known for advocating 'non-reductive physicalism': a non-**dualist** view of human persons in which our minds and our capacity to relate to God are features of our physical brains and bodies.[89] As described in Chapter 2, she also holds a non-interventionist view of divine action in which God acts by determining the outcomes of otherwise indeterminate quantum events. In relation to religious belief and experience, this means that ideas of God or plans for action might come into our minds by means of the processes described by CSR, and then God acts at the level of quantum events in the brain, to influence our responses to these ideas and plans.[90]

Murphy explains in a footnote that her attempt to appropriate Boyer's account of CSR is part of a larger project to defend the Christian tradition against the rival 'modern scientific naturalist tradition'.[91] She follows Alasdair MacIntyre's account of the encounter between different traditions, in which one tradition can prove itself superior to a rival by addressing the rival tradition's questions more successfully than the rival itself can.[92] On the assumption that CSR offers the best current naturalistic explanation of religion, Murphy therefore thinks that

> to defend the Christian tradition it is necessary either to show that CSR's explanations fail or that we can happily accept a lot of them as partial explanation and incorporate them in a helpful way into our own theological world view.[93]

She therefore attempts to show that CSR offers a good but incomplete account, which 'can handily be *complemented* by a

---

[88]Tyrrell, *Through Scylla and Charibdis*, p. 207, quoted by Murphy, 'Cognitive Science and the Evolution of Religion', p. 271.

[89]For example, Nancey Murphy, *Bodies and Souls, or Spirited Bodies?* (Cambridge: Cambridge University Press, 2006).

[90]Murphy, 'Cognitive Science and the Evolution of Religion', pp. 274–5.

[91]Ibid., pp. 265–6, note 1.

[92]Alasdair MacIntyre, *Whose Justice? Which Rationality?* (London: Duckworth, 1988), chs. 17–19.

[93]Murphy, 'Cognitive Science and the Evolution of Religion', pp. 265–6, note 1.

theological account of the development of religion'.[94] Her main aim is apologetic, but her apologetic strategy depends on developing a constructive theological account which can incorporate CSR and make better sense of its findings than a naturalistic account can.

However, is her chosen theological account up to the task? Tyrrell does affirm that 'Christ is the final and fullest revelation of God'.[95] However, he also insists that revelation is primarily an inner experience. As Delia Candelario argues, this tends to drive a wedge between the subjective experience of revelation and its expression in scripture and Christian tradition.[96] The result, in Murphy's hands, is that inner revelatory experiences assume a central role in the theological dialogue with CSR. This has two consequences.

First, to achieve her own stated aim, she must show that naturalistic CSR accounts of such experiences may be accurate, but are incomplete in themselves and need to be complemented by an account of a spiritual impulse 'from above'. It is clear enough why Christian theologians might say this. It is less clear why Boyer, from the perspective of his own naturalist tradition, ought to recognize this incompleteness or acknowledge that CSR needs the addition of quantum-level divine action in the brain. But this is what Murphy has to show, if the Christian tradition is going to win the MacIntyrean contest she sets up between it and scientific naturalism.

The second consequence is that the voice of the Christian tradition plays a rather limited role in the dialogue Murphy sets up with CSR. Now, Murphy's account is set out only briefly in a short essay, and if it were developed more fully, perhaps that voice could be heard more fully and clearly. But on the strength of this essay, the kind of theological dialogue with CSR proposed by Murphy appears to have limited scope for being informed by the scriptures and the Christian community's ongoing reflection on them. So although I have described her account as an example of my third type of science–theology encounter, it may be at risk of drifting towards type 2.

---

[94]Ibid., p. 277, emphasis in original.
[95]Candelario, 'George Tyrrell and Karl Rahner', p. 48.
[96]Candelario, 'George Tyrrell and Karl Rahner'.

4.5 The science of religion and the hermeneutics of suspicion: Type 4

Gregory Peterson remarks that CSR is often 'seen as an inheritor of the Feuerbachian project to reduce religion to something else, whether it be psychology, class struggle or will-to-power'.[97] This remark refers to the seminal account of religion given by the nineteenth-century philosopher Ludwig Feuerbach, which has often been seen as a serious challenge to Christian faith and theology. However, not all theologians have seen Feuerbach as a threat. For the twentieth-century Protestant Karl Barth, he was in a strange sense almost an ally: Barth saw his challenge as a valuable critique and corrective for Christian theology. In light of Peterson's remark, Barth's engagement with Feuerbach could perhaps offer, not an exact parallel, but a rough model for a theological engagement with the scientific study of religion in which the agenda is set by the voice of the Christian tradition. In this section I shall outline a proposal for how this might work.

While Barth's engagement with Feuerbach varies and develops through his theological career,[98] his main focus is on Feuerbach's book *The Essence of Christianity* and his so-called reduction of theology to anthropology.[99] Feuerbach sees religion as a projection of human nature and values onto infinity: 'the divine being is nothing else than the human being ... freed from the limits of the *individual* man.'[100] As Cumming puts it, 'Humanity creates God, as it were, in its own image.'[101] Rather than challenging this account of religion, Barth *agrees* with it, and makes use of it in various ways. One is to

---

[97]Peterson, 'Evolutionary/Cognitive Theories of Religion', p. 547.

[98]For detailed accounts of these changes and developments, see John Glasse, 'Barth on Feuerbach', *Harvard Theological Review*, 57, no. 2 (1964), pp. 69–96; Manfred H. Vogel, 'The Barth-Feuerbach Confrontation', *Harvard Theological Review* 59, no. 1 (1966), pp. 27–52; Richard Paul Cumming, 'Revelation as Apologetic Category: A Reconsideration of Karl Barth's Engagement with Ludwig Feuerbach's Critique of Religion', *Scottish Journal of Theology* 68, no. 1 (2015), pp. 43–60.

[99]Glasse, 'Barth on Feuerbach', p. 73.

[100]Ludwig Feuerbach, *The Essence of Christianity*, trans. George Eliot (Amherst, MA: Prometheus, 1983 (1841)), p. 14, quoted by Cumming, 'Revelation as Apologetic Category', p. 46, emphasis in original.

[101]Cumming, 'Revelation as Apologetic Category', p. 46.

criticize the nineteenth-century Protestant theology that he and his contemporaries inherited early in the twentieth century. According to Barth, Feuerbach's account correctly describes this theology. By taking human experience as the starting point for theology, he argues, nineteenth-century Protestants allowed themselves to be backed into an 'apologetic corner';[102] if we try to talk about God in that way, we shall really only be talking about ourselves.

Feuerbach's account also informs Barth's theological critique of religion.[103] Feuerbach's view of religion as human projection lies behind Barth's critique of religion as a futile human attempt to gain knowledge of God out of our own resources. According to Barth this is simply impossible, because God is God while we are finite and sinful creatures. The only way we can know God is if God reveals Godself to humanity, which God has done in the person of Jesus Christ. For Barth, Christian theology must *begin* from faith in this self-revelation of God in Christ, and if it does so, Feuerbach's sceptical question about religion as a projection of human experience simply does not arise.[104]

What might a theological engagement with evolutionary, cognitive and neuroscientific studies of religion look like, if it was modelled on Barth's engagement with Feuerbach? It could take very seriously the sceptical challenges to religious belief that authors like Bloom and Braddock base on these scientific studies – though theologians working in this way could well also raise critical questions about the scientific studies or their interpretation.[105] It might agree that such sceptical challenges undermine apologetic arguments based on CSR or neuroscience, such as those surveyed earlier. Theologians taking this approach might say that it is not

---

[102]Karl Barth, *Theology and Church: Shorter Writings 1920–1928*, trans. Louise Pettibone Smith (London: SCM, 1962), p. 227.

[103]Barth, *Church Dogmatics*, vol. 1.2, pp. 40–1, 297–325; see Cumming, 'Revelation as Apologetic Category', pp. 46–9.

[104]Barth, *Church Dogmatics*, vol. 4.3.1, pp. 72–86; Vogel, 'The Barth-Feuerbach Confrontation', pp. 44–8. Note that Barth's theological critique of religion should not be read simply as an exclusivist assertion of Christianity's superiority to other religions, not least because his critique also applies to Christianity as a religion. See Cumming, 'Revelation as Apologetic Category', p. 48.

[105]They might wish to raise similar critical questions to those of Markus Mühling, *Resonances*, pp. 92–7.

theology's business to try and argue apologetically for Christian faith on the basis of scientific evidence or data about the natural world. Instead, Christian theologians should begin with God's self-disclosure in Jesus Christ, to which the Scriptures witness. Then Braddock's sceptical conclusion, that we should suspend judgement about religious beliefs unless we have independent reasons for holding them,[106] becomes irrelevant, as Feuerbach's challenge did for Barth. For this kind of theological approach, Christian beliefs flow from a prior commitment of faith, which cannot be proved (or for that matter disproved) by 'independent reasons'. However, this approach might also criticize the assumption, which seems to be implied by many of the sceptical challenges, that faith is first and foremost about holding propositional beliefs. The propositions of Christian faith (e.g. 'Jesus Christ is God's revelation to humanity') cannot be separated from a richly textured web of communal worship, practice, narrative and belief.

An obvious objection to this approach is that it is based on a circular argument. It simply *presumes* there is a God who is revealed in Jesus Christ, which is precisely what the sceptical challenge calls into question. Barth considers a similar objection to his discussion of Feuerbach, and answers: 'Exactly!'[107] In his account, theology is faith seeking understanding, and its appropriate method is to 'believe *in order* to understand'.[108] He acknowledges that this form of theological reasoning is, in a sense, circular, but insists that it is a virtuous, not a vicious, circle. Some science and theology scholars, of course, would thoroughly object to this approach: Arthur Peacocke, for example, explicitly rejects it.[109] But there is quite wide support for the ideas that theology is faith seeking understanding, and that the purpose of theological engagement with science is not to prove the truth of Christian faith, but to develop the understanding of a faith held on other grounds. Robert John Russell is just one

---

[106]Braddock, 'Debunking Arguments and CSR'.
[107]Barth, *Church Dogmatics*, vol. IV.3.1, p. 86.
[108]In Latin, '*credo ut intelligam*'; ibid., p. 85. Here, Barth refers to the mediaeval theologian Anselm of Canterbury.
[109]Peacocke, *Paths from Science Towards God*, pp. 31–2.

example of a science and theology scholar who describes his work in this way, as we saw in Chapter 2.[110]

However, even if we agree with Barth about believing in order to understand, the approach I have outlined might seem closer to a type 5 than type 4 exercise. In other words, it might seem to leave no room for theology to be informed by scientific voices. Again, a similar criticism has often been made of Barth's theology: that it 'isolate[s] itself from general cultural awareness. ... It must remove itself to an island of grace and burn all the bridges'.[111]

Whether or not this is a fair criticism of Barth (and there are reasons to think that it is not),[112] the approach I have outlined offers a range of possibilities for a critical and constructive type 4 engagement with scientific studies of religion:

(1)   The critical questions and challenges raised by these studies might not only perform the ground-clearing function discussed earlier, making the case for a type 4 approach, but have a helpful ongoing *critical and corrective* function for theological work of this type. For example, some CSR scholars have discussed the concept of 'theological incorrectness': the tendency of cognitive mechanisms to generate beliefs that thoughtful theological reflection will see as overly anthropomorphic or unsatisfactory in other ways. By giving an account of why believers' minds might be predisposed to form such beliefs, CSR could inform a theological critique of inadequate forms of belief.[113]

(2)   Scientific findings might have a limited but valuable *constructive* contribution to make to theology, particularly theological anthropology. Barth once likened scientific and philosophical understandings of the human to 'an interesting commentary on a text which must first be known and read for itself if the commentary is to be intelligible and

---

[110]Russell, 'Quantum Theory and the Theology of Non-Interventionist Objective Divine Action', pp. 579–95 (p. 584).

[111]Vogel, 'The Barth-Feuerbach Confrontation', p. 49.

[112]See Nigel Biggar, *The Hastening That Waits: Karl Barth's Ethics* (Oxford: Clarendon, 1993), pp. 147–61; for a response to Vogel specifically, see Cumming, 'Revelation as Apologetic Category', pp. 50–9.

[113]Murphy, 'Cognitive Science and the Evolution of Religion', pp. 275–6.

useful'.[114] In other words, scientific understandings can only disclose 'phenomena' of the human; the reality of what it is to be human can only be known through God's revelation in Christ. But if that is accepted, there could be a good deal to learn from scientific 'commentary' which might help us understand this reality more fully.

(3) This theological perspective offers possibilities for Christian *dialogue* with other traditions, perspectives and disciplines. This will not be apologetic, in the sense of defending the claims of Christian faith, but those engaged in the dialogue might discover insights they share and things they can learn from one another.[115] This theological perspective maintains that 'the life of Jesus Christ really reveals God',[116] but the God who is revealed in Jesus Christ is free to reveal Godself wherever and however God chooses. Therefore it should not surprise Christians to find that insights they have reached on theological grounds are at least partly shared by others on other grounds. Nor should it surprise them if others are able to remind them of things they should have known, or to help them understand their own tradition better. For example, cognitive science and neuroscience generally assume a non-dualist view of brain and mind. Dialogue with these scientific voices can and should prompt Christians to ask whether their own tradition really supports a dualistic view of body and soul, as both Christians and their critics often assume.[117]

(4) Recognizing shared insights might also lead Christians to make common cause with their dialogue partners about shared concerns. For example, in the context of cognitive science and neuroscience, Christians might share with others a concern to resist reductive views of the human mind and person. And when theological thinking extends to *ethical*

---

[114]Barth, *Church Dogmatics*, vol. 3.2, p. 122.
[115]Cf. Ibid., pp. 277–8 and 'The Christian Understanding of Revelation', in R. G. Smith (ed.) and E. M. Delacour and Stanley Godman (trans.), *Against the Stream* (London: SCM, 1954), pp. 228–9.
[116]Glasse, 'Barth on Feuerbach', p. 88.
[117]See Messer, *Theological Neuroethics*, pp. 117–22.

questions raised by cognitive science and neuroscience, the range of shared concerns on which Christians may be able to make common cause with others could be considerable.[118]

4.6 Conclusion

This chapter has surveyed various types of engagement between Christian theology and the evolution, cognitive science and neuroscience of religion. Many of the conclusions of previous chapters have been reinforced by this discussion, although there are some new findings in this chapter which may nuance or modify those earlier conclusions.

In my first type of encounter, only the scientific voice or voices contribute to an understanding of religious belief, practice and experience. Discussion of this type raised the issue of naturalism in the scientific study of religion. I distinguished between methodological and ontological naturalism, and noted a recent debate among theologians about whether Christians should support methodological naturalism in scientific research. However, whatever the outcome of this debate, methodological naturalism in the scientific study of religion does not justify the ontologically naturalist conclusion that *only* naturalistic accounts of religion are valid.

Interestingly, not all type 1 accounts of the scientific study of religion are religiously sceptical. Justin Barrett's proposal for a CSR-based 'universal natural theology' is an attempt to defend belief in God purely on the basis of scientific evidence, without referring to scripture or other sources of revelation. Taken by itself, this is best understood as a type 1 exercise, which does not involve any *dialogue* between the voices of science and Christian tradition. However, Barrett seems to see it as one part of a larger and more methodologically diverse project. In this larger project, it may be complemented by other types of engagement such as his 'confessional natural theology', which would encourage dialogue

---

[118]For reflection on a range of ethical issues raised by neuroscience, see Ibid.

between those voices. Even as part of a larger project, though, I have suggested that it may have some difficulties and dangers.

In the fifth type, scientific voices play no part in shaping theological understanding, often because the domains of scientific and Christian voices are so sharply separated that they do not interact. In previous chapters, I argued on theological grounds that this is an unsatisfactory position; in relation to scientific studies of religion, it may also be a difficult one to maintain. However, a reflection on Peter Harrison's historical analysis of the shifting meanings of 'science' and 'religion' raised the question whether a theological dialogue about the 'scientific' study of 'religion' would result in such a distorted understanding that it is better not attempted. Even if this is not the case for this topic, this historical reflection raises the possibility that it could, in theory, be true for others. Although there are good theological reasons for rejecting type 5 in general, there could in principle be particular dialogues that would confuse rather than illuminate, which would be better avoided.

All of the middle types in my classification (types 2, 3 and 4) are genuine attempts at dialogue between scientific voices and a voice of the Christian tradition. However, not all are equally promising. In relation to the scientific study of religion, it becomes particularly clear that type 2 approaches are vulnerable to the sceptical challenges and debunking arguments produced by some type 1 authors. Type 3 approaches, depending less on scientific voices to shape theological understanding, are less vulnerable to these challenges. However, as in previous chapters, one of the examples I discussed (Nancey Murphy's engagement with CSR) proved to be at risk of drifting towards type 2.

As an example of type 4, I suggested a theological engagement with scientific studies of religion modelled on Karl Barth's engagement with Ludwig Feuerbach's account of religion. Barth was able to treat Feuerbach as an ally (up to a point) in criticizing problematic trends in modern theology. In the same way, I have proposed that a type 4 approach could welcome, rather than fearing, sceptical challenges and debunking arguments based on scientific studies of religion. These challenges might expose the weaknesses of unsatisfactory forms of theological engagement (such as apologetic arguments that depend heavily on scientific evidence or theory) and perform an ongoing corrective and constructive role for Christian theology. However, a problem that commentators note with Barth's treatment of Feuerbach is also a danger for the type 4 approach I have outlined: theological reasoning in this mode could become sealed off from scientific and other voices, drifting from type 4 to type 5.

Like previous chapters, this one has suggested that both the third and fourth types of approach offer rich possibilities for theological engagement with scientific studies of religion, but both have characteristic dangers. The second type, once again, has proved more problematic. In general, the first and fifth types have once again been ruled out, but this is less clear-cut than in previous chapters. I have noted examples of type 1 and 5 arguments that could have more significant parts to play in various ways in theological engagements with the scientific study of religion.

5

Concluding reflections

Using the five types

CHAPTER SUMMARY

This final chapter draws together conclusions about the typology and offers further reflections on the ways it may be used in theological engagements with the natural sciences. The first two sections draw together conclusions from the three test cases explored in Chapters 2–4. I conclude that the typology has proved a useful tool in organizing and clarifying a range of debates in science and theology, and can avoid the dangers of oversimplification and **reductionism,** for which older typologies have been criticized. These test cases have also suggested some conclusions about how theological engagements with science *should* be conducted. In general, I reject the types at either end of the scale (1 and 5), though some type 1 accounts may have valuable critical roles to play, and there may be rare cases where type 5 is appropriate. Of the middle three types, in which both scientific and Christian voices contribute to our understanding, I find type 2 problematic in various ways. Types 3 and 4 are preferable, but both have characteristic dangers, so each is needed to check and correct the other. In Paul DeHart's words, they form a 'mutually stabilizing pair'.

Sections 5.3 and 5.4 extend the dialogue to consider the contributions of other voices. Section 5.3 explores various roles that philosophical voices might play in theological engagements

> with the sciences. Section 5.4 explores what creative and artistic voices might contribute, focusing on poetry, as seen particularly in the work of Christopher Southgate. The chapter concludes with some suggestions about how readers might use the typology in their own study and research.

In Chapter 1, I set out a typology of approaches to the encounters of Christian theology with the natural sciences. The central question the typology addresses is how much, and what, scientific insights should contribute to theological understanding. I suggested that we can think of this (in a simplified way) as a conversation involving two voices, a voice of the Christian tradition and the voice of a scientific discipline. The question then becomes: If we wish to understand ourselves and the world in relation to God, what contribution to that understanding should we expect from each voice? I identified five possible answers to that question, corresponding to five types of theological engagement with science:

1) Only the scientific voice contributes, and the contribution of the Christian tradition is denied or dismissed.

2) Both voices contribute, but the scientific voice plays the predominant role in shaping the dialogue and addressing the questions. The claims of the Christian tradition must be adjusted where necessary to fit an account whose shape and content are determined by science.

3) Both voices contribute, and neither predominates in shaping the dialogue or answering the questions.

4) Both voices contribute, but the voice of the Christian tradition plays the predominant role in shaping the encounter and addressing the questions.

5) Only the voice of the Christian tradition contributes, and the contribution of the scientific voice is denied or dismissed.

Chapters 2–4 illustrated and tested this typology by applying it to detailed surveys of three current topics from across the range of science and theology debate: divine action in the light of contemporary physics (Chapter 2), the problem of natural evil in the light of biological evolution (Chapter 3), and the significance of the evolution, cognitive science and neuroscience of religion for Christian faith and theology (Chapter 4). In Sections 5.1 and 5.2 I shall summarize the main conclusions we can draw from these three test cases. Then I shall briefly consider the role of other voices in the conversation, besides those of science and the Christian tradition. Finally, I shall offer some suggestions about how the typology could be used by those working in the science and theology field.

5.1 Describing and analysing debates in science and theology

First, we can draw some conclusions about the use of the typology to describe and understand debates in the science and theology field. As I explained in Chapter 1, in a single chapter a comprehensive survey of the literature on any of these topics was not feasible, but I have surveyed a representative sample of the literature on each. These surveys have proved the typology to be a useful tool in organizing a large and diverse literature and giving some shape to complex debates.

But do these gains come at the cost of oversimplifying or flattening out the debates, obscuring their nuance and complexity, or forcing diverse positions into reductive categories? As I noted in Chapter 1, this is a standard criticism of older typologies such as Ian Barbour's: they turn the complex and diverse social practices of 'science', 'religion' and 'theology' into simple, reified categories, and ask how the reified entities labelled 'science' and 'religion' (or 'theology') relate to one another. If this is true, it is easy to see how it results in reductive, oversimplified and distorting accounts.

However, the scheme I have presented in this book reflects a very different approach. This approach attends to *particular* debates and theological encounters with particular scientific disciplines or research areas. It asks what those scientific disciplines or areas of research contribute to theological understanding in the various contributions to those debates. This should make it sensitive to the diversity, nuance and complexity of the debates that it is used to study. Indeed, it can make that diversity and nuance *more* visible. For example, in Chapter 2, using the typology to analyse the divine action debate highlighted the diversity in both the Divine Action Project (DAP) and the 'theological turn'. This made it easier to avoid treating either the DAP or the theological turn as a uniform category.

Various kinds of diversity are found in these debates. Scientific disciplines and research fields are diverse, and raise different kinds of question for theological understanding. The use of three contrasting test cases in Chapters 2–4 has shown that the typology can easily accommodate that diversity. John Perry and Sarah Lane Ritchie point out another form of diversity: theology, like science, has various disciplines and sub-disciplines (such as philosophical, systematic, moral and practical theology, each with its various branches). Different theological disciplines will ask different questions and engage differently with scientific voices.[1] So far in this book I have not emphasized this form of theological diversity, but it is reflected to some extent in the different theological issues raised in Chapters 2–4. Again, because the typology encourages us to attend to the particular features of specific debates, it can readily accommodate this kind of diversity. This is, however, a reminder that not all theological disciplines or topics require the same kind of engagement with scientific voices, and some may not require any engagement with science.[2] We shall need to bear this in mind in the next section, when we consider how theological engagements with scientific voices *ought* to be set up.

This also suggests that the typology is better used to describe particular accounts, arguments or contributions to particular debates than *authors* as a whole. The whole body of a scholar's work may be complex, diverse and varied in its approach. Some science and theology scholars do work predominantly in one type: this was true, for example, of Arthur Peacocke, discussed in Chapters 2 and 4.[3] However, others may vary in the approaches they use. They may judge that different debates and theological questions require different types of engagement with scientific voices.

---

[1]Perry and Ritchie, 'Magnets, Magic, and Other Anomalies', pp. 1064–93 (pp. 1084–9).
[2]Ibid., p. 1087.
[3]In this section and the next, when I mention authors discussed in earlier chapters, I shall not generally reproduce the references to their publications. To follow up these authors' works, readers are referred back to the fuller discussions and references in Chapters 2–4.

I need hardly say that Christian traditions, their theological approaches and perspectives are also diverse. This means, as I acknowledged in Chapter 1, that my rather catch-all category of 'a voice of the Christian tradition' will take different forms in the work of scholars from different branches of Christianity. This need not mean that those differences are obscured or suppressed, provided we do not make the mistake of imagining that the typology tells us everything there is to know about a particular author's account. Diverse accounts of a particular topic might be classified into the same type: for example, the three examples of the theological turn in the divine action debate (Chapter 2) represent Orthodox, Catholic and Pentecostal Christian traditions. What they have in common is the weight each gives to the voice of their own Christian tradition in shaping an understanding of divine action in dialogue with scientific voices.

The test cases also suggest some interesting conclusions about the extreme positions on the typology (types 1 and 5) in particular.

Type 1 denies any role to voices of the Christian tradition in forming theological understanding. Many of my examples were atheist, anti-religious or religiously sceptical: Victor Stenger in Chapter 2, Richard Dawkins in Chapter 3 and those who interpret scientific studies of religion in ontologically naturalist ways in Chapter 4. Not all type 1 arguments, though, are atheist or sceptical. For example, Justin Barrett's cognitive science of religion (CSR)-based 'universal natural theology', discussed in Chapter 4, is an attempt to argue for theistic belief from scientific evidence alone without appealing to sources of revelation such as sacred texts. Whether this has its own problems and dangers will be discussed in the next section, but it does underline the point that type 1 approaches are not always atheist or sceptical.

Conversely, type 5 can take the form of a rejection of scientific insights, as in the creationist rejection of evolution (Chapter 3). However, it does not have to. For example, as we saw in Chapter 2, Stephen Jay Gould's proposal of non-overlapping magisteria (NOMA) was motivated by *respect* for both science and religion. For Gould, each should respect the boundaries of the other's territory, which in effect means that science will play no part in shaping theological insights.

For some theologians, type 5 might represent a general policy about the (non-)engagement of theology with science, but for others the diversity of science–theology encounters again comes into play here. Peter Harrison's historical perspective on scientific studies of religion (Chapter 4) raises the possibility that refusing to engage with a scientific voice might be a decision about that particular research field and that particular dialogue, not a general reluctance to engage theologically with science.

To summarize the conclusions of this section:

- The typology is a useful tool for organizing and clarifying complex debates in the science–theology field.
- It need not oversimplify or distort these debates or obscure their nuances, provided that (1) it is used as a way of attending carefully to *particular* issues and debates, rather than making generalizations about how 'science' and 'theology' relate; (2) it is used primarily to describe particular accounts or arguments rather than scholars and (3) we do not imagine that it tells us everything we need to know about a particular position or account.
- Various kinds of diversity are evident in theological engagements with the sciences, and the typology can help us to remain aware of these forms of diversity.
- In particular, the extreme positions, which rule out any contribution of one or other voice to theological understanding, turn out to be diverse in some surprising ways.

5.2 Evaluating and guiding debates in science and theology

The typology is not only a tool for describing and analysing debates in the science and theology field. I have also used it to evaluate the debates surveyed in Chapters 2–4, and to draw some conclusions about how Christian theology *should* engage with scientific voices.

5.2.1 The extreme positions: Types 1 and 5

Type 1 approaches rule out any contribution from voices of the Christian tradition. Some of the religiously sceptical arguments I placed in that category in Chapters 2–4 turned out to have serious flaws. For example, Victor Stenger's and Richard Dawkins's attacks on religious belief (Chapters 2 and 3) are directed against a 'God of the gaps' who is a cause among causes in the physical world. To the extent that this is not what the Christian tradition understands by 'God', these attacks will be irrelevant to Christian faith. Type 1 accounts of this sort may, however, offer a valuable critical perspective on some Christian theological accounts. For example, some contributions to the divine action debate do tend to treat God's action as a cause among causes in the physical world, as we saw in Chapter 2. Anti-religious accounts like Stenger's may serve as a warning about the dangers of doing so. Or again, sceptical arguments based on scientific studies of religion, such as Paul Bloom's and Matthew Braddock's (Chapter 4), may demonstrate the dangers of theological accounts that rely too heavily on evidence from the same scientific studies.

For those wishing to give a theological account of Christian understanding, it would on the face of it seem odd to exclude the voice of the Christian tradition. One reason for doing so might be apologetic, as in Justin Barrett's CSR-based 'universal natural theology' (Chapter 4): an attempt to argue for theistic belief on the basis of reason and scientific evidence alone, in a way that could convince any rational person. However, this type of apologetic is vulnerable to sceptical challenges such as Bloom's and Braddock's, which point to non-theistic interpretations of the same evidence. Barrett tries to counter such challenges by shifting the burden of proof onto the sceptics. His defence, though, relies on a particular philosophical position (the 'reformed epistemology' of Alvin Plantinga and others), so any successful challenge to that position would seriously undermine his apologetic argument.

At the other end of the scale, *type 5* approaches exclude any role for scientific voices in forming theological understanding. In Chapters 2–4, I was generally sceptical about the value of this type of encounter. Versions such as creationism (Chapter 3), which reject scientific voices on religious grounds, have well-known problems. I also suggested in Chapter 2 that versions such as NOMA, which respect both voices but confine them to separate territories, are generally theologically problematic, and probably unworkable for at least some specific debates. In some fields, such as the divine action debate, it seems impossible to maintain the clear boundary that NOMA requires, and for a tradition which values the physical world as God's creation, it would seem odd if the empirical study of that world had *nothing* to contribute to theological understanding.

However, if type 5 is unsatisfactory as a general policy, that does not necessarily mean it should always be ruled out. For one thing, as Perry and Ritchie remark, not all theological fields need to be 'science-engaged'.[4] Also, as I suggested with reference to Peter Harrison in Chapter 4, a particular scientific field could conceivably be set up in such a way that engagement with it would more likely distort and obscure theological understanding than illuminate it. In that case, non-engagement might be the best policy, at least for the time being. Such cases, though, would be rare, and that judgement should be made only as a last resort.

5.2.2 The middle positions: Types 2, 3 and 4

In *type 2*, the scientific voice plays the predominant role in setting the agenda for the conversation and shaping the account that emerges. Perhaps the most impressive example of this type is the DAP (Chapter 2).[5] The DAP has some important achievements to its credit, such as clarifying and 'stabilizing' the terminology for discussing God's action in the world, and classifying a range of options for considering divine action theologically.[6]

However, giving priority to the scientific voice in these dialogues can have far-reaching consequences for theological understanding. In the case of the DAP, it means that a particular scientific theory such as quantum mechanics may be given a powerful role in stipulating how God can and cannot act in the world. It also makes theology vulnerable (at least in principle) to the kind of despairing conclusion reached by Nicholas Saunders, that there is no scientifically plausible account of divine action in the world.[7] Since faith in a God who acts in the world is at the heart of the Christian tradition, this is a radical possibility to contemplate. To many theologians in that tradition, it will also seem presumptuous

---

[4]Perry and Ritchie, 'Magnets, Magic, and Other Anomalies', p. 1087.
[5]As I noted in Chapter 2, however, not all contributions to the DAP could be described as type 2, even if that was where the project's centre of gravity lay.
[6]See Wildman, 'The Divine Action Project, 1988–2003', pp. 31–75.
[7]Saunders, *Divine Action and Modern Science*, p. 215.

to stipulate, on the grounds of human scientific understanding, whether and how God can act in the world.

In the discussion of evolution and natural evil (Chapter 3), a type 2 approach can lead to some similarly radical revision of traditional Christian understandings of God: in particular, God's power, goodness or both. While some authors such as Wesley Wildman present this radical revision simply as a corrective to modern distortions of the Christian tradition, I argued in Chapter 3 that it seems to involve abandoning some core Christian convictions and practices. Many theologians working in that tradition will consider the cost of such radical surgery too high.

Type 2 approaches often have a strong apologetic motivation.[8] One example is Arthur Peacocke's approach of 'inference to the best explanation' (Chapter 4), in which he argues that a variety of evidence about the world is best explained by the existence of God. There was also a strong apologetic strand in early accounts of the 'neurotheology' proposed by Eugene d'Aquili and Andrew Newberg. However, I argued in Chapter 4 that such apologetic approaches – especially those like d'Aquili and Newberg's, which are based on scientific studies of religion – are vulnerable to sceptical challenges of the sort made by Bloom and Braddock. These challenges offer a '**hermeneutics** of suspicion', as Gregory Peterson puts it.[9] They not only point to naturalistic explanations for phenomena such as religious belief and experience; they also call into question the reliability of the cognitive processes which lead us to see the existence of God as the best explanation for such phenomena.

I have suggested that type 2 approaches may be theologically problematic. Ironically – in view of the authority they give to scientific voices – it can also be argued that they do a disservice to *science*. What I mean is this. Broadly speaking, the modern natural sciences have achieved their extraordinary successes by restricting themselves to questions about physical cause and effect within the

---

[8]See Chapter 1, Section 1.5 and n. 45 for an explanation of what I mean by 'apologetic', and why the work of scholars such as Peacocke can be described in this way.

[9]Peterson, 'Are Evolutionary/Cognitive Theories of Religion Relevant for Philosophy of Religion?', pp. 545–57 (p. 550).

confines of the natural world.[10] Most theologians who engage with the natural sciences would agree that this self-limitation is entirely appropriate for scientific enquiry. If so, to expect scientific voices to play a leading role in supporting belief in God or shaping a theological understanding of the world may be to ask of them what they are not equipped to deliver. It may fail to respect their integrity as intellectual practices of a particular kind.

In the *third type* of approach, neither the voice of the Christian tradition nor the scientific voice dominates. The authors of type 3 accounts seek, in Christopher Southgate's words, 'to give full weight to the Christian doctrinal tradition', but also 'to learn from science about the way things really are'.[11] This allows greater scope for theology to be shaped by its characteristic sources: the scriptures and the churches' traditions of reflection and practice grounded in those scriptures. I have suggested that type 2 approaches may have theological costs that many Christian theologians would regard as too high; type 3, by giving greater weight to the voices of Christian traditions, avoids some of the costs and problems I have identified with type 2.

However, in Chapters 2–4 I argued that the examples of type 3 I surveyed have some dangers of their own. For instance, in Southgate's discussion of evolution and theodicy, '[learning] from science about the way things really are' means that scientific evidence plays a part in shaping our understanding of God's goodness and good purposes. I suggested in Chapter 3 that in doing this, he is looking to science for theological insights that it is not equipped to supply. As I noted in Chapter 1, the question raised by the typology is not only *how much* but *what* theology ought to learn from the natural sciences. I have suggested that Southgate's answer to the 'what' question shares some of the problems of type 2.

I have expressed a similar concern about some of the other accounts I have placed in type 3: they tend to drift towards type 2 and share some of its problems. In Chapter 2, for example, we saw how Sarah Lane Ritchie welcomes the 'theological turn' in the

---

[10]In this they are following the advice of the advice of the seventeenth-century philosopher Francis Bacon, *The Advancement of Learning* (London: Cassell, 1893 (1605)), Book 2, 7.7. Online at http://www.gutenberg.org/files/5500/5500-h/5500-h.htm (accessed 8 April 2019).

[11]Southgate, 'God's Creation Wild and Violent', pp. 245–53 (p. 247).

divine action debate as a corrective to the DAP, but argues that we still need an account of the 'causal joint' by which God interacts with the material world. I questioned how the kind of account for which Ritchie calls would avoid the problems she identifies with the DAP. I expressed a similar concern in Chapter 4 about Nancey Murphy's theological engagement with CSR.

By giving voices of the Christian tradition the predominant role in shaping theological understanding, *type 4* accounts can avoid the dangers I have associated with type 3. Scholars who work in this way may be suspicious of science-based apologetics, or attempts to defend the credibility of the Christian faith in the context of a scientific view of the world. They may therefore welcome the sceptical challenges outlined in type 1 as useful critiques of such apologetic accounts. In Chapter 4 I suggested that a type 4 engagement with scientific studies of religion could make theological use of the sceptical arguments of Bloom and Braddock, somewhat as Karl Barth used Ludwig Feuerbach's critique of religion and theology.

Scholars working in this way might see theology as 'faith seeking understanding', echoing Barth.[12] On this view, the main purpose of the science–theology encounter will be to discover how scientific findings or theories can contribute to a theology that springs from a commitment of faith, is grounded in the scriptures and is formed by the churches' traditions of reflection on those scriptures.

This means, however, that type 4 has a characteristic danger of its own. This can be seen in a comment by Barth, whom I used as a model for type 4 approaches in Chapters 3 and 4: 'There is free scope for natural science beyond what theology describes as the work of the Creator. And theology can and must move freely where science which really is science … has its appointed limit.'[13] This looks very much like Stephen Jay Gould's NOMA, in which theology and science have different territories and the only interaction between them is to maintain the border. This suggests that type 4 approaches may be at risk of drifting towards type 5, in

---

[12]Cf. Karl Barth, *Anselm: Fides Quaerens Intellectum, Anselm's Proof of the Existence of God in the Context of His Theological Scheme*, trans. Ian W. Robertson (London: SCM Press, 1960).
[13]Barth, *Church Dogmatics*, ed. G. W. Bromiley and T. F. Torrance, 13 vols (Edinburgh: T & T Clark, 1956–75), vol. 3.1, p. x.

which theology becomes sealed off from any real engagement with natural science. In Chapter 3, I noted that Southgate sees this danger in my approach to evolutionary theodicy. I believe my account can avoid the risk, but I agree that the risk is a real one.

5.2.3 Summary

In general, I have argued that the extreme positions in my classification are unpromising approaches to developing an understanding of ourselves and the world in relation to God. However, there are exceptions to my suspicion of these approaches. Sceptical type 1 accounts may raise valuable critical questions about other, more overtly theological, types of encounter. Type 5 may be appropriate for some theological enquiries, in the sense that not all theology needs to engage with scientific voices. It could conceivably also be an appropriate response to some scientific research fields, though theologians should be wary of making this judgement.

The middle positions in my scheme all represent genuine dialogues between scientific voices and voices of the Christian tradition, but they vary widely in the ways those dialogues are set up. I have suggested that type 2, in which a scientific voice plays the dominant role, is a problematic way for theology to engage with science. Some of its problems are exposed by sceptical type 1 critiques. However, it would of course be open to someone who disagreed with this judgement to show that these problems do not arise, can be overcome or are outweighed by the advantages of this type.

I have taken a more positive view of types 3 and 4, because they allow greater scope for Christian theology to make use of its characteristic sources and methods. Perhaps both these types are needed within the 'ecology' of theological encounters with the natural sciences. Indeed, Southgate argues that different issues in science and theology *require* different approaches. As we saw in Chapter 3, he believes that evolutionary theodicy demands a type 3 approach because on this question, 'robust science encounters theology at its most tentative'.[14] By contrast, he thinks, other issues would require a type 4 approach.[15]

---

[14]Southgate, 'Cosmic Evolution and Evil', pp. 147–64 (p. 156).
[15]Southgate, 'Response with a Select Bibliography', pp. 909–30 (pp. 916–20).

Perhaps Southgate is right, but we have also seen that each of these types has its own characteristic dangers. In particular, each is prone to drift towards one of the more problematic types: type 3 towards type 2, and type 4 towards type 5. Each is well placed to draw attention to the other's characteristic danger, as I argued in Chapter 3. It could even be that in most debates in science and theology, each type *needs* the challenge and critique of the other to help it avoid its own characteristic problems. Perhaps types 3 and 4 make up what Paul DeHart, in a different but related context, has called a 'mutually stabilizing pair' of theological approaches.[16]

5.3 Other voices: Philosophy

I emphasized in Chapter 1 that the voices of scientific disciplines and the Christian tradition are not the only ones in the conversation. Although it has been helpful to concentrate for most of the book on the relationship between these two kinds of voice, it would be a mistake to forget the contributions of others. In this section I shall discuss the diverse roles that philosophical voices play in theological engagements with the natural sciences. In the next section I shall reflect on a neglected aspect of the science–theology field, the contributions that creative and artistic voices might make.[17]

In an exploration of neuroscience, evolution and theology, Markus Mühling makes a strong claim for the importance of a philosophical voice: 'Natural science and theology can only fruitfully lead a dialogue if philosophy and especially natural philosophy are taken into account. Therefore, there can be no dialogue without a "trialogue".'[18] Mühling, like many authors, thinks of this as a dialogue between 'natural science' and 'theology',

---

[16]DeHart, *The Trial of the Witnesses*, p. 217.

[17]Of course, it is an oversimplification to treat these as separate voices. As the following discussion makes clear, for much of Christian history the 'voice of the Christian tradition' was in part a philosophical one, and it has also very often been a voice expressed through artistic media. Philosophy and science have been equally intertwined at some times in Western history. Still, there is value in treating these as distinct voices and asking what their distinctive contributions to theological understanding might be.

[18]Mühling, *Resonances*, p. 225.

in which (he claims) 'philosophy' is needed as a third partner in the conversation. This is an image I have tried to avoid in this book, for reasons explained in Chapter 1. Therefore my question uses a somewhat different image: In forming a *theological* understanding of ourselves and the world, what role(s) should be played by philosophical voices, alongside those of scientific disciplines and a Christian tradition? Nevertheless, Mühling's remark is a helpful reminder that the question needs to be asked.

But what do we mean by 'philosophy'? As we have already seen, the idea of philosophy, theology and science as separate disciplines which might interact with one another is surprisingly recent.[19] According to Peter Harrison, in ancient Greece the study of natural phenomena was part of philosophy, but philosophy itself was primarily concerned with the 'art of living' or the 'good life'.[20] Likewise, the term 'theology' was not much used before the later Middle Ages to refer to Christian doctrine, and its meanings and uses shifted greatly from ancient through mediaeval to modern times.[21] Our familiar disciplinary boundaries developed in modernity, as academic work became increasingly specialized and professionalized, and the empirical sciences separated from philosophy to form their own disciplines.[22]

It would be a near-impossible task to define the discipline of philosophy, following this process of specialization and separation of disciplines, in a way that most philosophers would agree to. Murphy suggests that a major part of philosophy's activity in the modern era has been to act as 'the arbiter of the rational status of other disciplines'.[23] So epistemology becomes its core, and it develops branches labelled 'philosophy *of*' other disciplines – science, religion and so on. But this looks more like a description of the so-called 'analytic' tradition in contemporary philosophy than the 'continental' tradition.[24] In any case, Murphy argues that this

---

[19]So also Nancey Murphy, 'On the Role of Philosophy in Theology-Science Dialogue', *Theology and Science* 1, no. 1 (2003), pp. 79–93 (p. 80).

[20]Harrison, *The Territories of Science and Religion*, pp. 26–34.

[21]Ibid., pp. 17–18.

[22]Murphy, 'On the Role of Philosophy', p. 80; see Harrison, *Territories*, chs. 5, 6.

[23]Murphy, 'On the Role of Philosophy', p. 80.

[24]For one philosopher's account of the analytic/continental divide in philosophy, see Neil Levy, 'Analytic and Continental Philosophy: Explaining the Differences',

view has become so problematic that it should be discarded, and as we shall see, she proposes a different kind of role for philosophers.

In fact, philosophical theories, concepts, ideas and methods play such diverse roles in science–theology encounters that it would be very difficult to classify these roles systematically. Instead, I shall simply give various examples of contributions made by philosophical voices, some drawn from the debates surveyed in Chapters 2–4.

5.3.1 Premodern voices: Questioning the categories

I have already suggested that in premodern times, it would not have made sense to think of philosophy and theology in a modern way as separate disciplines that might interact. Before the modern age, my question about the contributions of philosophical voices to theological understanding, alongside the voices of scientific disciplines and the Christian tradition, would probably have seemed odd and puzzling. The voice of the Christian tradition *was* in part a philosophical voice, and there were not distinct scientific voices in the modern sense. This can be seen particularly in the work of Thomas Aquinas, who brings Aristotle's thought together with a Christian tradition rooted in the Bible and mediated through earlier Christian thinkers like Augustine.[25] Therefore, in accounts which use premodern Christian sources extensively, much of the philosophical contribution may be intertwined with the voice of the Christian tradition. When Denis Edwards draws on Aquinas in his account of divine action, Aquinas's synthesis of Aristotelian and biblically grounded Christian thought makes an important contribution to Edwards's own discussion.[26] However, this is not the only way in which philosophical voices enter Edwards's discussion; for example, he also draws on William Stoeger's philosophical reflections on the laws of nature.[27]

Metaphilosophy 34, no. 3 (2003), pp. 284–304. Murphy observes that the continental tradition has been less influential in the English-language science and theology literature: 'On the Role of Philosophy', p. 91, n. 4.

[25]See MacIntyre, *Whose Justice? Which Rationality?*

[26]See, for example, Edwards, *How God Acts*, pp. 80–4.

[27]Ibid., pp. 84–7; cf. Stoeger, 'Contemporary Physics and the Ontological Status of the Laws of Nature', in Russell et al. (eds) *Quantum Cosmology and the Laws of Nature*, pp. 207–31.

5.3.2 Frameworks and chaperones

For many authors, philosophy is needed to provide a framework which sets the terms of the encounter between scientific and Christian voices. This can be seen in one way in the work of scholars who use Alfred North Whitehead's 'process philosophy' as the metaphysical framework for their work on science and theology.[28] For some, this involves radical revision of classical Christian God-talk, since Whitehead regarded the doctrine of a transcendent, all-powerful Creator as a tragic mistake on the part of Christianity.[29] In its place he proposed a 'dipolar' God with 'primordial' and 'consequent' sides to his nature; God's consequent nature depends for its completion on God's experience of the physical world.[30] The notion of a God who is in some sense dependent on the natural world for the completion of God's nature seems a radical departure for Christian theology. Yet it is one that many authors have been prepared to take, because they have found Whitehead's metaphysics an attractive way of 'fusing ... religion and science ... into one rational scheme of thought', as he puts it.[31] Some theologians who have used Whitehead's thought, however, have attempted to revise or 'stretch' his framework to make it more consistent with key aspects of Christian belief.[32]

Whitehead's process theology is not the only metaphysical scheme that functions as a governing framework for the encounter of science and theology. Philip Clayton argues that some kind of metaphysical framework is needed to provide a 'level playing field' or 'provide a neutral context within which claims [about science

---

[28]See, for example, David Ray Griffin, 'Interpreting Science from the Standpoint of Whiteheadian Process Philosophy', in Clayton and Simpson (eds), *The Oxford Handbook of Religion and Science*, pp. 453–71; also Joseph A. Bracken, 'Contributions from Philosophical Theology and Metaphysics', in Clayton and Simpson (eds). *The Oxford Handbook of Religion and Science*, pp. 345–58. Whitehead's thought can be found, for example, in Alfred North Whitehead, *Process and Reality*, ed. David Ray Griffin and Donald W. Sherburne (New York: Free Press, 1978).

[29]Whitehead, *Process and Reality*, p. 342.

[30]Ibid., part 5, ch. 2.

[31]Ibid., p. 15.

[32]For example, Bracken, 'Contributions from Philosophical Theology and Metaphysics', pp. 354–7.

and theology] could be evaluated'.[33] In Clayton's view, the best such framework is panentheism, in which the whole of created reality is 'in' God, though God is more than the whole of created reality.[34] In a more modest way, Robin Collins argues that one of the most important contributions that the philosophy of science can make to the science and religion field is 'helping provide a framework for understanding what the sciences are telling us about the world that is friendly to religion yet true to science'.[35] For Collins, this means rejecting reductionist frameworks for understanding natural phenomena, and thinking in a different way about how and why the world is intelligible to human beings.

The use of philosophy to provide a framework setting the terms of the encounter has been described as giving philosophers the role of 'cultural magistrates' or 'chaperones' for the meeting of science with theology.[36] Authors such as Nancey Murphy and Philip Hefner reject this 'chaperoning' role, and advocate different and more modest roles for philosophy in this encounter. A number of the authors surveyed in earlier chapters use philosophy in a variety of such ways.

5.3.3 'Trialogues' and toolboxes

For some, a philosophical contribution functions as another voice in the dialogue, alongside those of scientific disciplines and the Christian tradition, without dictating the terms of the dialogue. One example is Markus Mühling, who uses the phenomenology of Husserl, Merleau-Ponty and others – a school of thought from the continental rather than analytic tradition – as one voice in a dialogue with neuroscience and a theological understanding of revelation.[37] This

---

[33]Philip D. Clayton, *God and Contemporary Science* (Edinburgh: Edinburgh University Press, 1997), pp. 153, 156.

[34]Ibid., ch. 4.

[35]Robin Collins, 'Contributions from the Philosophy of Science', in Clayton, *The Oxford Handbook of Religion and Science*, pp. 328–44 (p. 328).

[36]Murphy, 'On the Role of Philosophy', p. 82, citing Philip Hefner, 'Eluding the Chaperones: A Conversation with Phil Hefner, Part II', *Research News & Opportunities in Science and Theology* 2, no. 2 (October 2001), p. 6.

[37]Mühling, *Resonances*.

enables him (among other things) to critique common neuroscientific assumptions about the role of the brain in cognition, and to develop an alternative view of revelation in dialogue with neuroscience.

For others, philosophical concepts, ideas or arguments serve as tools which can help in developing particular accounts or approaches. One example, discussed in Chapter 4, is Justin Barrett's use of Thomas Reid's 'commonsense epistemology' and its development by Alvin Plantinga, which plays an important role in Barrett's defence of a CSR-based natural theology.[38] Another, from Chapter 2, is the way Amos Yong uses the metaphysics of the American pragmatist philosopher C. S. Peirce to re-think what is meant by laws of nature, thus creating space for his Pentecostal-charismatic account of divine action.[39]

5.3.4 Therapy, critique and clarification

Nancey Murphy, following Ludwig Wittgenstein, suggests that one important role for philosophy is 'therapeutic'. Drawing on the work of George Lakoff and Mark Johnson, she argues that much of our ordinary language is shaped by metaphors derived from our experience of embodied life in the world, but these metaphors can mislead us if they provide unspoken assumptions in our philosophical theories. For example, she argues that the epistemological debate between realists and anti-realists – a live issue for science and theology – is misconceived, because both sides in the debate are framed by an image of knowers looking out at the world through a 'veil of language'. This is a 'beguiling' but false picture, from which Wittgenstein's 'therapeutic' philosophy could help free us.[40]

More generally, authors in science and theology quite frequently use philosophical voices to play a critical and corrective role in dialogues between science and the Christian tradition. For example, I have used D. Z. Phillips's philosophical critique of theodicy to

---

[38]Barrett, *Cognitive Science, Religion, and Theology*, pp. 148–60.
[39]Amos Yong, *The Spirit of Creation: Modern Science and Divine Action in the Pentecostal-Charismatic Imagination* (Grand Rapids, MI: Eerdmans, 2011), pp. 118–32.
[40]Murphy, 'On the Role of Philosophy', pp. 84–90.

challenge some approaches to evolution and the problem of evil.[41] In a different way, Lisa Stenmark has shown how feminist philosophy can challenge 'objectivist' epistemologies which are very influential in the science and theology field, which understand reliable knowledge as objective, universal and value-neutral. Instead, she argues, feminist epistemology emphasizes that knowers are always situated in particular social contexts and knowledge arises in relational contexts. This, she argues, calls for a different way of understanding and practising the 'science and religion discourse'.[42]

Finally, philosophical voices may play various constructive roles, particularly in clarifying concepts, ideas or arguments, or helping those involved to understand what is going on in science–theology encounters.[43] For example, Nancey Murphy has used the concept of a 'research programme', developed by the philosopher of science Imre Lakatos, to understand what was going on in her own work and that of other science and theology scholars like Ian Barbour and Arthur Peacocke.[44] Philip Clayton, though he differs from Murphy on various issues, has used Lakatos's notion of research programmes in a similar way.[45] More recently, Murphy has drawn on Alasdair MacIntyre's argument that knowledge and reasoning are always located in particular traditions, and his account of how different traditions may engage one another, to shape her philosophical and theological response to CSR.[46] She presents her evaluation of CSR as part of a defence of the Christian tradition against the rival tradition of 'modern scientific naturalism'.[47] However, it could be asked whether this use of MacIntyre's thought as a guiding framework for a science–theology encounter comes close to the 'chaperoning' role she has criticized elsewhere.

---

[41]See Messer, 'Natural Evil after Darwin', pp. 139–54; Phillips, *The Problem of Evil and the Problem of God*.

[42]Stenmark, 'Going Public: Feminist Epistemologies, Hannah Arendt, and the Science-and-Religion Discourse', in Clayton, *The Oxford Handbook of Religion and Science*, pp. 821–34.

[43]See Murphy, 'On the Role of Philosophy', pp. 82–3.

[44]Nancey Murphy, 'Theology and Science within a Lakatosian Program', *Zygon* 34, no. 4 (1999), pp. 629–42.

[45]Philip Clayton, 'Shaping the Field of Theology and Science: A Critique of Nancey Murphy', *Zygon* 34, no. 4 (1999), pp. 609–18.

[46]Murphy, 'Cognitive Science and the Evolution of Religion', pp. 265–77.

[47]Ibid., pp. 265–6, note 1.

5.3.5 Conclusion

I have not tried to offer a systematic classification of the parts philosophical voices may play in science–theology encounters, only to illustrate the range and variety of ways in which they may be involved. Even this unsystematic survey should be a reminder that when using the typology to analyse the ways in which theology engages with scientific voices, it is also important to ask what part philosophical voices might be playing in these encounters. Also, when setting up a dialogue between a Christian tradition and some area of natural science, it is important to consider which philosophical voices should be drawn into the dialogue, what they might contribute and how they might help to shape its outcomes.

5.4 Other voices: Poetry

In a sense, this book has mostly been about particular ways in which scripture, tradition, reason and experience interact to form a theological understanding of ourselves and the world in relation to God. The natural sciences could be thought of, roughly speaking, as particular ways of using reason to understand aspects of the world, generally informed in one way or another by the carefully structured and controlled forms of experience that we call 'experiment'. Much of the book has been about how these forms of reason and experience might interact with Christian traditions, which are rooted in the scriptures and in the history of Christian communities' responses to those scriptures in their faith, reason and practice. In this chapter the discussion has broadened to include some of the ways in which philosophical reason might interact with the voices of scientific disciplines and Christian traditions to shape theological understanding.

However, there are other ways in which human experience is captured, mediated, reported and reflected upon, in which scripture is read, interpreted and responded to, and in which Christian traditions are represented and expressed. In particular, creative imagination plays a vital part in all of these activities. A dialogue that shapes theological understanding requires imagination and creativity – as almost any intellectual activity does in some way or other. Voices which give expression to creative imagination might therefore have something distinctive and important to contribute to dialogues between the natural sciences and the Christian tradition.

The creative arts have a massive, varied and complex role in theology, and it would be far too big a task to try and give a general account of that role in the closing pages of a short book.[48] Instead, I shall consider a few specific examples of how creative and artistic voices might contribute to theological dialogues between Christian traditions and the natural sciences. To narrow the focus still further, I shall concentrate on one particular art form: poetry. Probably the leading figure in the engagement of poetry with the science and theology field is Christopher Southgate, who is both a science and theology scholar and a poet. The following account draws heavily on his own work and his use of other poets.[49]

5.4.1 Different ways of knowing

To begin with the point I have just made: there are different ways of knowing the world and ourselves, and scientific ways are not the only ones. This is expressed in the first stanza of Southgate's poem 'Knowing':

My first experiment on living tissue.
Pick a new leaf – copper beech –
chop into chloroform. Watch
as the hydrophobic pigments
leach to solvent.
A longer lesson is to follow those leaves
from bud-burst,
each morning after lovemaking,
savour their tints from pale strawberry
to old, tannic claret
and on into honey and on into rusted gold.[50]

---

[48]For one recent perspective, see Jeremy S. Begbie, *A Peculiar Orthodoxy: Reflections on Theology and the Arts* (Grand Rapids, MI: Baker Academic, 2018).

[49]Some of the following draws on Christopher Southgate, 'Poetry and Science' (unpublished lecture, St Stephen's Church, Exeter, October 2018). I am most grateful to Professor Southgate for sharing a copy of this lecture with me and for permission to cite it. Some of the same themes are explored in Christopher Southgate, 'Nature's Million-fuelèd Bonfire: Thoughts on Honest Poetic Contemplation', *Theology in Scotland* 24, no. 1 (2017), pp. 7–20.

[50]Christopher Southgate, 'Knowing', in *Easing the Gravity Field: Poems of Science and Love* (Nottingham: Shoestring Press, 2006), pp. 54–5.

In theological engagements with the natural sciences, it can be tempting to limit what we say theologically to what can be conceived or imagined scientifically. In effect, that was my criticism of some contributions to the Divine Action Project (Chapter 2). Creative and imaginative voices, including poetic ones, can remind us that there are other ways of seeing the world, and what needs to be said theologically is not limited to what the sciences can investigate and theorize.

Yet Southgate is more concerned to emphasize what poetic and scientific ways of knowing have in common. The remaining stanzas of 'Knowing' interweave scientific and imaginative ways of seeing breaking waves on the shore at dusk and the sky at night, and conclude that humans 'have to be known' not only by our culture but by our evolutionary history and connection with the natural world:

> the open hazard of the savannah –
> eagles screaming overhead, baboons jeering,
> the need for survival, the need for tribes ...[51]

This emphasis on what science and poetry have in common leads to a second theme.

5.4.2 Honest contemplation

According to Southgate, both scientists and poets are involved in *contemplation* of the world. This requires an 'intense attention to natural phenomena', a willingness to look in unusual places and be open to surprising findings, and a confidence that intense attention will enable us to discover 'deep truths about the world'.[52] He cites the nineteenth-century poet Gerard Manley Hopkins as someone whose intense contemplation of the world was expressed in both contributions to scientific journals and poetic lines like these:

> As kingfishers catch fire, dragonflies dráw fláme;
> ...
> Each mortal thing does one thing and the same:
> Deals out that being indoors each one dwells;

---

[51]Ibid., p. 55.
[52]Southgate, 'Poetry and Science', n.p.

Selves – goes itself; *myself* it speaks and spells,
Crying *Whát I do is me: for that I came.*[53]

Southgate maintains that scientific and poetic knowing 'enrich each other ... we are better contemplaters, better poets, for allowing science to tell us deep things about the world we try and attend to'.[54]

One way he thinks science can make poets better contemplators is to keep them honest. It is tempting for Christians in particular to focus on the beauty of the world and ignore its darker side: the struggle, suffering and destruction which Darwinian evolution powerfully discloses. Again Southgate cites Hopkins as an 'honest nature contemplative', whose poetry reflects this ambivalence.[55] Among more recent examples, he cites both the poetry and the autobiographical writing of R. S. Thomas.[56] This honest contemplation of nature's ambivalence informs Southgate's own work on evolutionary theodicy (Chapter 3), illustrated in various publications by his reflections on watching predators, such as orcas or peregrines, hunting.[57]

5.4.3 Expressing the inexpressible

Poetic voices can sometimes give vivid expression to theological ideas, and can help us grasp those ideas more clearly and fully. In his work on evolutionary theodicy, Southgate has drawn on the mediaeval theologian John Duns Scotus's idea of *haecceitas*: the

---

[53]Gerard Manley Hopkins, 'As Kingfishers Catch Fire', online at http://www.gutenberg.org/cache/epub/22403/pg22403-images.html (accessed 11 November 2019), emphasis in original.

[54]Southgate, 'Poetry and Science', n.p.

[55]For example, Gerard Manley Hopkins, 'That Nature Is a Heraclitean Fire and of the Comfort of the Resurrection', online at https://www.poetryfoundation.org/poems/44397/that-nature-is-a-heraclitean-fire-and-of-the-comfort-of-the-resurrection (accessed 10 April 2019).

[56]Southgate, 'Poetry and Science', n.p., citing R. S. Thomas, *Autobiographies*, trans. Jason Walford Davies (London: Phoenix, 1997); R. S. Thomas, 'Rough', in *Collected Poems 1945–1990* (London: J.M. Dent, 1993), p. 286. This theme is explored more fully in Southgate, 'Nature's Million-fuelèd Bonfire'.

[57]For example, Southgate, *The Groaning of Creation*, pp. ix–x; Southgate, 'God's Creation Wild and Violent', pp. 245–53 (pp. 245–46).

particular God-given identity of an individual creature. Hopkins was deeply influenced by Scotus's thought, and this idea is expressed powerfully in several of his nature poems, including the lines quoted earlier from 'As Kingfishers Catch Fire'.[58]

Sometimes poets can help articulate theological ideas that we struggle to capture with more prosaic language, because theology speaks of matters that are beyond human understanding, which stretch human language to – and beyond – its limits. Again, an example can be found in Southgate's work on evolutionary theodicy. In this discussion, a question arises whether animals who suffer and whose lives are unfulfilled in this world will be fulfilled at the eschaton (in God's promised good future). If so, what might that fulfilment look like, for both predators and prey? This is something we can only speculate about in the most tentative way. To help him imagine what a future fulfilment for animals could look like, Southgate turns to James Dickey's poem 'The Heaven of Animals', in which the poet imagines a heaven where there is still predation, but no pain or lasting death.[59]

5.4.4 Reason, emotion, and a moral and spiritual vision

Poetry can also give voice to the part the emotions play in science and in theological engagements with science.[60] It might seem surprising to introduce the emotions, since it is often assumed that they have no part to play in rational scientific enquiry. But the reality of scientific practice is more complex and untidy than this, and as Southgate puts it, 'feeling and … yearning' are often part of the process.[61] Apart from anything else, what motivates a good deal of scientific research – and a good deal of theological engagement with science – is that the questions *matter* in some way. The fact that they matter has something to do with the emotions. Poetry is

---

[58]Southgate, *The Groaning of Creation*, p. 63.

[59]Ibid., pp. 88–9. Dickey's poem can be found at https://www.poetryfoundation.org/poems/42711/the-heaven-of-animals (accessed 9 October 2019).

[60]See Margaret Boone Rappaport and Christopher Corbally, 'Tracing Origins of Twenty-First Century Ecotheology: The Poetry of Christopher Southgate', *Zygon* 53, no. 3 (2018), pp. 866–75.

[61]Southgate, 'Poetry and Science', n.p.

one way this 'mattering' can be articulated; poetic voices can engage our emotions and help us see how, and why, the questions matter.[62]

Moral engagement, too, can be provoked and encouraged by poetry. The moral dimensions of theology's engagement with the sciences have not been foregrounded in this book, but they are there. Southgate and I agree, for example, that our differing accounts of evolution and theodicy will have moral implications for humans' treatment of other animals. We agree that humans have moral obligations in respect of animals, but we disagree about what those obligations are, in ways related to our differences about theodicy (Chapter 3).[63] Theology's engagement with neuroscience (Chapter 4), too, includes diverse moral issues, some of which I have explored elsewhere.[64]

More generally, the practice of science and its impacts on the world have inescapable moral implications. Good poetry does not generally moralize, but it can express a moral vision and draw attention to matters of moral concern. Southgate again cites R. S. Thomas as one recent example.[65] Another is his own poem 'Crick, Watson, and the Double Helix'. In this work he uses the highly structured 'villanelle' form to express both the excitement of the groundbreaking discovery of the DNA double-helix structure in the 1950s, and the growing moral ambiguity of what follows from that discovery:

A single insight made the Book of Life cohere,
Sent two men shouting into a Cambridge bar.
More slowly there steals upon us the power, the fear.[66]

Finally, there is what might be called a spiritual vision. Christian theology is shaped by Christian practices of prayer, worship and

---

[62]For one expression of this, see Christopher Southgate, 'Taboo', in *Easing the Gravity Field*, pp. 60–2.

[63]See Southgate, *The Groaning of Creation*, ch. 7; Neil Messer, 'Evolution, Animal Suffering and Ethics: A Response to Christopher Southgate', in Andrew Linzey and Clair Linzey (eds), *The Routledge Handbook of Religion and Animal Ethics* (Abingdon: Routledge, 2018), pp. 337–46.

[64]Messer, *Theological Neuroethics*.

[65]Southgate, 'Poetry and Science', n.p., citing inter alia R. S. Thomas, 'Roger Bacon', in *Selected Poems* (London: Penguin, 2003), p. 129.

[66]Christopher Southgate, 'Crick, Watson, and the Double Helix', in *Easing the Gravity Field*, p. 53.

spiritual life – or their absence – and theology informed by the voices of the natural sciences is no exception. Poetry is one among many art forms which can point to the spiritual vision that shapes theological understanding, and so make those connections more explicit.[67]

5.4.5 Conclusion

I have used poetry (and the work of Southgate in particular) as just one focused example of the way in which creative and imaginative voices may also play a part in dialogues between the natural sciences and a Christian tradition. Other art forms such as prose literature, visual arts or music could equally well have been considered, and each would have had different and distinctive things to bring to the dialogue.

Of course, there is nothing uniquely authoritative about these voices. The imaginative visions they articulate and the ways they influence theological engagements with science are open to questioning and critique, like other voices in the dialogue. For example, I agree with Southgate about the importance of honest contemplation of the natural world, but we differ about where that contemplation should lead us in thinking theologically about evolution and suffering. But the main conclusion of this section is that such voices may help us notice things in the dialogue that we would otherwise miss, or see issues in new ways, or express things that would otherwise be hard to put into words.

5.5 Using the typology

Although some of the discussions in this book may seem rather abstract, I stated in Chapter 1 that one of its main aims is to be a useful resource to students and researchers in the science and theology field. In this final section, I shall conclude the book with some brief suggestions for how the book, and the typology it presents, may be used by those working in the field.

---

[67]For one expression of this see Christopher Southgate, 'Sancte et Sapienter', in *Easing the Gravity Field*, pp. 56–7.

5.5.1 Understanding and engaging with work in science and theology

I have suggested that the typology, and the discussions I have built onto it, can be used by anyone wishing to clarify and understand the shape of debates on a wide range of science and theology topics. The typology can help us classify the contributions to these debates, position them in relation to one another and engage critically with those contributions. Readers who wish to do these things could ask various questions about any particular contribution to the topics they are exploring:[68]

1. What type in the typology does this contribution or argument represent? In other words, how much do the voices of the Christian tradition and the relevant scientific discipline(s) contribute to theological understanding of the topic? Is one voice excluded? Does one predominate in setting the agenda and shaping theological understanding? Or do the voices have more or less equal roles?

2. The question is not only how much but *what* each voice contributes. What kind of thing is each voice expected or allowed to say in the dialogue? Are there things that the voices are *not* expected or permitted to say?

3. What are the characteristic dangers or weaknesses of the type of engagement that this contribution represents? How far does this example avoid the characteristic dangers of its type, and how does it do so?

4. Try to dissect each voice in the dialogue a little: for this author, what are the components of 'the voice of the Christian tradition'? What role does scripture play? How is it related to the history of Christian faith, reason and practice? Whose voices are *not* being heard in this account of how scripture should be read and the Christian faith practiced; for example, are the voices of women, the poor or non-European cultures sidelined or silenced? What

---

[68]These questions, and those in Section 5.5.2, arise from the conclusions drawn in Sections 5.1–5.4, and roughly follow the order of those sections.

scientific voices or disciplines are involved in the dialogue?
What ongoing controversies might there be within these
disciplines, and what bearing might those have on its
contribution to theological understanding? For example,
when scholars in the divine action debate propose ideas
of quantum divine action, how much do their proposals
depend on particular (and contested) interpretations of
quantum theory (see Chapter 2, Box 2.1)? In discussions of
theology and evolution, does an author's account depend
on a particular interpretation of evolutionary theory such as
the 'extended evolutionary synthesis' (EES; see Chapter 3,
Box 3.2)?

5. What part do philosophical voices play in shaping
theological understanding in this account? How do
philosophical voices relate to those of the sciences and
Christian traditions involved in the dialogue? What are the
advantages and pitfalls of the ways in which philosophy is
being used?

6. What imaginative, emotional, moral or spiritual visions
shape the theological understanding that this author is
developing? Where do these visions come from, and how
are they expressed in the account? Are creative, artistic or
imaginative voices explicitly brought into the conversation,
or are these perspectives expressed more indirectly? How
adequate are they to the task of helping shape a theological
understanding?

5.5.2 Planning new work in science and theology

The typology and the way it is set out in this book are also intended
to offer a guiding framework for students and researchers beginning
new projects in science and theology. Those planning new projects
or seeking to engage with issues and debates in science and theology
could consider the following questions:

1. Where do you want to position your work, and why? I
have proposed that types 3 and 4 are generally the most
satisfactory forms of theological engagement with the

sciences, and both are needed: in DeHart's words, they form a 'mutually stabilizing pair'. If you have chosen one of these types, why have you chosen the one you have, and how do you plan to avoid its characteristic dangers? If instead you want to do something more like type 2, do you agree with my conclusions about the theological costs and dangers of this type? If so, how will you minimize or offset those costs and dangers? Will the extreme types (1 and 5) make any contribution to your project, and if so, what?

2. How do you understand 'the voice of the Christian tradition'? What parts will scripture and tradition play in your account, and how will they relate to one another? What sources in particular will contribute to your account: what biblical texts, narratives or themes, what theologians or theological movements and what aspects of Christian faith and practice might help to shape your theological understanding?

3. Recall that the question is not just *how much* each voice contributes, but *what*. What kinds of thing will you seek to learn from the scientific voice or voices in your dialogue, what will you *not* seek to learn from these voices, and why? What kinds of contribution should come from the voice of the Christian tradition, and what kinds of contribution should this voice *not* be expected to make?

4. What role or roles will philosophical voices play in shaping your theological understanding? How will these philosophical voices be related to the others in your dialogue? What kinds of philosophical voices will be included, and where will you find them?

5. What imaginative vision and metaphors shape your understanding of your topic? How will you give expression to that vision and those metaphors: will creative and artistic voices help you do so? When your imaginative vision and guiding metaphors are made explicit, how adequate are they to the task of developing your account? How might they need to be stretched, extended or reshaped?

6. What moral or spiritual visions shape your understanding and account? Where do these come from: have they been

shaped by particular spiritual practices, moral commitments, exemplars, experiences or theories? Again, when they are made explicit, how adequate are they? Are there ways in which they too might need to be stretched, extended or re-shaped?

5.6 And finally …

I have tried to show in this book how a relatively simple classification scheme, which can be expressed in a page or two, can help us understand and critically evaluate a wide range of complex debates in the science and theology field. I have also tried to show how this scheme can guide new work in the field, helping students and researchers position their own work, making explicit their own understanding of what they aim to achieve and how. Although the typology is relatively simple, I have suggested that it can open up a range of more nuanced and fine-grained questions about both existing work and new projects. It is therefore offered to those seeking to engage theologically with the natural sciences, in the hope that they will find it helpful in structuring and guiding their ongoing work.

GLOSSARY AND LIST OF ABBREVIATIONS

Note: This glossary offers brief definitions of specialized or technical terms and abbreviations that appear in the text. Many terms are defined in text boxes in earlier chapters: in those cases I have not repeated the definitions here, but have referred the reader to the relevant boxes.

Apologetics the attempt to give a rational argument ('apology' or *apologia*) for religious faith.

Atonement in Christian theology, the work of Jesus Christ (particularly in his death on the cross) to reconcile humanity and the world to God.

Burden of proof in philosophy, the obligation to justify a claim that one makes.

Causal joint a mechanism, or aspect of reality, through which God acts in the world.

Charismatic related to the work or the gifts of the Holy Spirit; a form of Christianity whose worship and theology place great emphasis on the work and the gifts of the Spirit.

Christology the branch of Christian theology concerned with the person of Jesus Christ.

CMI creative mutual interaction (see Section 1.6).

Compatibilism see Box 2.3.

Contingent not necessary; refers to a state of affairs that could have been otherwise, or a being that might not have existed.

CSR the cognitive science of religion (see Section 4.1.1).

CTNS the Center for Theology and the Natural Sciences, Berkeley, California.

DAP the Divine Action Project (see Section 2.4).

Deism a theological view that developed in the late seventeenth and eighteenth centuries, in which God has created the cosmos but does not act or intervene in its working.

Determinism see Box 2.3.

Dualism   a system of thought which divides reality (or some aspect of reality) into two fundamental categories. For example, cosmic dualism sees good and evil as the two fundamental realities of the cosmos; substance dualism in the philosophy of mind sees the human person as composed of physical matter and non-physical mind.

EEG   electroencephalography.

EES   the Extended Evolutionary Synthesis (see Box 3.2).

Efficient cause   see Box 2.3.

Epistemology   the theory of knowledge, or the branch of philosophy concerned with knowledge and justified belief.

Eschatology   the branch of theology concerned with the 'last things', the end of the present age and the life of the world to come.

Eschaton   in theology, the end of the present world or age.

Essentialism   in philosophy, the view that objects are defined and given their identity by their essences or essential characteristics. More generally, the mistake of regarding a social, cultural or intellectual construct as something with a fixed identity or essence.

Evangelicalism   a tradition of Protestant Christian faith and theology that has a high view of the authority of the Bible and is generally conservative in doctrine and ethics.

Fall   in Christian theology, traditionally, the sin of Adam and Eve, through which humanity became alienated from God; contemporary theology may use 'fall' or 'fallenness' to refer to humanity's or the world's alienation from God without presupposing a literal fall of an historical Adam and Eve. (See also: Original sin.)

Fideism   reliance on faith alone, and rejection of reason, as a way to attain religious truth.

Final cause   see Box 2.3.

fMRI   functional magnetic resonance imaging.

Formal cause   see Box 2.3.

GDA   General divine action (see Section 2.2).

HADD   hypersensitive agency detection device (see Box 4.1).

Hermeneutics   the study or theory of interpretation.

IBE   inference to the best explanation (see Section 4.3.1).

Immanence   see Box 2.4.

Incarnation   in Christian theology, God the Son becoming human in the person of Jesus Christ.

Incompatibilism   see Box 2.3.

Indeterminism   the view that natural processes are not fully deterministic.

Instrumentalism   see Box 2.2.

Macroscopic   in quantum physics, the world at a larger scale than the microscopic (q.v.), including the scale of humans and the objects in our everyday environment.

Material cause   see Box 2.3.

Materialism   in philosophy, the theory that matter is the only fundamental reality, and all things can be explained in terms of matter and its interactions.

MCI   minimally counter-intuitive (see Box 4.1).

Metaphysics   the branch of philosophy concerned with the nature of being and reality.

Microscopic   in quantum physics, the scale of atoms and subatomic particles.

MRI   magnetic resonance imaging.

Natural evil   evil in the world that is not caused by human wickedness or sin.

Natural theology   see Box 4.3.

Naturalism   see Box 4.2.

Necessitarianism   see Box 2.2.

Niche (evolutionary)   see Box 3.2.

NIODA   non-interventionist objective divine action (see Section 2.4.1).

NOMA   non-overlapping magisteria (see Section 2.3.2).

Omnipotence   the divine attribute of being all-powerful.

Omniscience   the divine attribute of possessing complete and perfect knowledge.

Ontology   the philosophical study of being and concepts related to being.

Original sin   in Christian theology, traditionally the first sin of Adam and Eve, which caused the 'fall' of humanity. In contemporary theology, it may refer to the present human condition of being alienated from God from the very beginning of our existence, without presupposing that this condition was literally caused by the first sin of an historical Adam and Eve.

Panentheism   a philosophical and theological position which holds that all created things are 'in' God, but God is more than the sum of all created things.

Pantheism   a philosophical and theological position which identifies God with the cosmos or all that exits.

Pathogen   a disease-causing microorganism.

Postliberalism   a diverse theological movement of the late twentieth and twenty-first centuries, associated with Hans Frei, George Lindbeck and others. Among other things, it emphasizes the particularity of Christian (as well as other) traditions of faith, and depicts Christian theology as an activity that must be firmly located in the church, its traditions and practices.

Pneumatology   the branch of Christian theology concerned with the Holy Spirit.

Primary cause   see Box 2.3.

QM-NIODA   quantum mechanical non-interventionist objective divine action (see Section 2.4.1).

Reductionism   in philosophy or science, the idea that more complex entities or phenomena can be reduced to (i.e. completely described or defined in terms of) simpler ones. Varieties of reductionism include 'ontological', 'causal' and 'methodological'.

Regularism   see Box 2.2.

Reification   the fallacy of treating an abstract concept as if it were a concrete object or event.

Resurrection   in Christian theology, the action of God to raise the dead to new life; specifically, the raising of Jesus to new life following his death by crucifixion.

SDA   special divine action (see Section 2.2).

Secondary cause   see Box 2.3.

Spandrel   in evolutionary theory, a non-adaptive by-product of other adaptive changes.

Teleology   the study of ends, goals or purposes, or an explanation of something in terms of its ends, goals or purposes.

Theism   belief in a God or gods, often specifically belief in a God who has created the cosmos and is active in the world (by contrast with deism (q.v.)).

Theodicy   in philosophy and theology, an attempt to give an account of the justice or goodness of God in the face of the existence of evil.

Thomism   a tradition of theology and philosophy with its roots in the thought of Thomas Aquinas.

Transcendence   see Box 2.4.

Wave function   see Box 2.1.

BIBLIOGRAPHY

Achtner, Wolfgang and Ulrich Ott. 'Protestantism and Mysticism from the
Perspective of Neuroscience'. *Theology and Science* 11, no. 3 (2013),
pp. 208–23.

Alston, William P. 'Divine Action, Human Freedom, and the Laws of
Nature'. In Robert John Russell, Nancey Murphy and C. J. Isham
(eds), *Quantum Cosmology and the Laws of Nature: Scientific
Perspectives on Divine Action*, 2nd edn. Vatican City: Vatican
Observatory/Berkeley, CA: Center for Theology and the Natural
Sciences, 1999, pp. 185–206.

Applegate, Kathryn. 'A Defense of Methodological Naturalism'.
Perspectives on Science and Christian Faith 65, no. 1 (2013), pp.
37–45.

Aristotle. *Metaphysics*, trans. W. D. Ross. Online at http://classics.mit.edu/
Aristotle/metaphysics.5.v.html (accessed 16 January 2019).

Atkins, Peter. *The Creation*. London: W. H. Freeman, 1981.

Atkins, Peter. 'Science and Atheism'. In Philip Clayton (ed.), *The Oxford
Handbook of Religion and Science*. Oxford: Oxford University Press,
2008, pp. 124–36.

Augustine, *Enchiridion*, Library of Christian Classics, vol. 7, trans. Albert
C. Outler. London: SCM, 1955. Online at http://www.ccel.org/ccel/
augustine/enchiridion.

Bacon, Francis. *The Advancement of Learning*. London: Cassell, 1893
[1605]. Online at http://www.gutenberg.org/files/5500/5500-h/5500-h.
htm.

Barbour, Ian G. *When Science Meets Religion*. San Francisco, CA:
HarperSanFrancisco, 2000.

Barbour, Ian G. 'On Typologies for Relating Science and Religion'. *Zygon*
37, no. 2 (2002), pp. 345–59.

Barrett, Justin L. *Cognitive Science, Religion, and Theology*. West
Conshohocken, PA: Templeton Press, 2011.

Barrett, Justin L. 'Cognitive Science of Religion: Looking Back, Looking
Forward'. *Journal for the Scientific Study of Religion* 50, no. 2 (2011),
pp. 229–39.

Barrett, Justin L. 'Cognitive Science of Religion and Christian Faith: How May They Be Brought Together?' *Perspectives in Science and Christian Faith* 69, no. 1 (2017), pp. 3–12.

Barth, Karl. *Against the Stream*, ed. R. G. Smith and trans. E. M. Delacour and Stanley Godman. London: SCM, 1954.

Barth, Karl. *Church Dogmatics*, eds G. W Bromiley and T. F. Torrance, 13 vols. Edinburgh: T & T Clark, 1956–75.

Barth, Karl. *Anselm: Fides Quaerens Intellectum, Anselm's Proof of the Existence of God in the Context of His Theological Scheme*, trans. Ian W. Robertson. London: SCM Press, 1960.

Barth, Karl. *Theology and Church: Shorter Writings 1920–1928*, trans. Louise Pettibone Smith. London: SCM, 1962.

Beauregard, Mario and Vincent Paquette. 'Neural Correlates of a Mystical Experience in Carmelite Nuns'. *Neuroscience Letters* 405 (2006), pp. 186–90.

Beauregard, Mario and Vincent Paquette. 'EEG Activity in Carmelite Nuns during a Mystical Experience'. *Neuroscience Letters* 444 (2008), pp. 1–4.

Begbie, Jeremy S. *A Peculiar Orthodoxy: Reflections on Theology and the Arts*. Grand Rapids, MI: Baker Academic, 2018.

Biggar, Nigel. *The Hastening That Waits: Karl Barth's Ethics*. Oxford: Clarendon, 1993.

Blocher, Henri. 'The Theology of the Fall and the Origins of Evil'. In R. J. Berry and T. A. Noble (eds), *Darwin, Creation and the Fall*. Nottingham: Apollos, 2009, pp. 149–72.

Bloom, Paul. 'Religious Belief as an Evolutionary Accident'. In Jeffrey Schloss and Michael J. Murray (eds), *The Believing Primate: Scientific, Philosophical, and Theological Reflections on the Origins of Religion*. Oxford: Oxford University Press, 2009, pp. 118–27.

Bolos Anthony and Kyle Scott. 'Reformed Epistemology'. In James Fieser and Bradley Dowden (eds), *Internet Encyclopedia of Philosophy* (n.d.). Online at http://www.iep.utm.edu/ref-epis/.

Bonhoeffer, Dietrich. *Letters and Papers from Prison*, eds Christian Gremmels et al. and trans. Isabel Best et al., Dietrich Bonhoeffer Works, 8. Minneapolis, MN: Fortress, 2010.

Boyer, Pascal. *Religion Explained: The Evolutionary Origins of Religious Thought*. New York: Basic Books, 2001.

Bracken, Joseph A. 'Contributions from Philosophical Theology and Metaphysics'. In Philip Clayton (ed.), *The Oxford Handbook of Religion and Science*. Oxford: Oxford University Press, 2008, pp. 345–58.

Braddock, Matthew. 'Debunking Arguments and the Cognitive Science of Religion.' *Theology and Science* 14, no. 3 (2016), pp. 268–87.

Breck, John. *Scripture in Tradition: The Bible and Its Interpretation in the Orthodox Church*. Crestwood, NY: St Vladimir's Seminary Press, 2001.

Brooke, John Hedley, Russell Re Manning and Fraser Watts, eds. *The Oxford Handbook of Natural Theology*. Oxford: Oxford University Press, 2013.

Calvin, John. *Institutes of the Christian Religion*, trans. Henry Beveridge. Grand Rapids, MI: Eerdmans, n.d.

Candelario, Ma. Delia A. 'George Tyrrell and Karl Rahner: A Dialogue on Revelation'. *Heythrop Journal* 50 (2009), pp. 44–57.

Cantor, Geoffrey and Chris Kenny. 'Barbour's Fourfold Way: Problems with His Taxonomy of Science-Religion Relationships'. *Zygon* 36, no. 4 (2001), pp. 765–81.

Cartwright, Nancy. *The Dappled World: A Study of the Boundaries of Science*. Cambridge: Cambridge University Press, 1999.

Catechism of the Catholic Church. Online at http://www.vatican.va/arc hive/ENG0015/_INDEX.HTM.

Charlesworth, Deborah, Nicholas H. Barton and Brian Charlesworth. 'The Sources of Adaptive Variation'. *Proceedings of the Royal Society B* 284 (2017), DOI: http://dx.doi.org/10.1098/rspb.2016.2864.

Clayton, Philip D. *God and Contemporary Science*. Edinburgh: Edinburgh University Press, 1997.

Clayton, Philip D. 'Shaping the Field of Theology and Science: A Critique of Nancey Murphy.' *Zygon* 34, no. 4 (1999), pp. 609–18.

Clayton, Philip D. *Adventures in the Spirit: New Forays in Philosophical Theology*, ed. Zachary Simpson. Minneapolis, MN: Fortress, 2008.

Clayton, Philip D., ed. *The Oxford Handbook of Religion and Science*. Oxford: Oxford University Press, 2008.

Clayton, Philip D. and Stephen Knapp. *The Predicament of Belief: Science, Philosophy, and Faith*. Oxford: Oxford University Press, 2011.

Collins, Robin. 'Contributions from the Philosophy of Science'. In Philip D. Clayton (ed.), *The Oxford Handbook of Religion and Science*. Oxford: Oxford University Press, 2008, pp. 328–44.

Cox, Brian and Jeff Forshaw. *The Quantum Universe: Everything that Can Happen Does Happen*. London: Penguin, 2012.

Crutchfield, James P., et al. 'Chaos'. In Robert John Russell, Nancey Murphy and Arthur Peacocke (eds), *Chaos and Complexity: Scientific Perspectives on Divine Action*, 2nd edn. Vatican City: Vatican Observatory/Berkeley, CA: Center for Theology and the Natural Sciences, 1997, pp. 35–48.

Cumming, Richard Paul. 'Revelation as Apologetic Category: A Reconsideration of Karl Barth's Engagement with Ludwig Feuerbach's Critique of Religion'. *Scottish Journal of Theology* 68, no. 1 (2015), pp. 43–60.

D'Aquili, Eugene G. and Andrew B. Newberg. 'The Neuropsychological Basis of Religions, or Why God Won't Go Away'. *Zygon* 33, no. 2 (1998), pp. 187–201.

D'Aquili, Eugene G. and Andrew B. Newberg. *The Mystical Mind: Probing the Biology of Religious Experience*. Minneapolis, MN: Fortress, 1999.

Darwin, Francis, ed. *The Life and Letters of Charles Darwin, Including an Autobiographical Chapter*, 3 vols. London: John Murray, 1887.

Dawkins, Richard. *The Selfish Gene*. Oxford: Oxford University Press, 1976.

Dawkins, Richard. *River Out of Eden: A Darwinian View of Life*. London: Phoenix, 1996.

Dawkins, Richard. *The God Delusion*. London: Black Swan, 2007.

Deane-Drummond, Celia. *Christ and Evolution: Wonder and Wisdom*. London: SCM, 2009.

Deane-Drummond, Celia. 'Perceiving Natural Evil through the Lens of Divine Glory? A Conversation with Christopher Southgate'. *Zygon* 53, no. 3 (2018), pp. 792–807.

DeHart, Paul J. *The Trial of the Witnesses: The Rise and Decline of Postliberal Theology*. Oxford: Blackwell, 2006.

Dennett, Daniel. *Breaking the Spell: Religion as a Human Phenomenon*. New York: Viking, 2006.

Edwards, Denis. *How God Acts: Creation, Redemption, and Special Divine Action*. Minneapolis, MN: Fortress, 2010.

Falcon, Andrea. 'Aristotle on Causality'. In Edward N. Zalta (ed.), *The Stanford Encyclopedia of Philosophy* (Spring 2015 Edition). Online at https://plato.stanford.edu/archives/spr2015/entries/aristotle-causality/.

Feuerbach, Ludwig. *The Essence of Christianity*, trans. George Eliot. Amherst, MA: Prometheus, 1983 [1841].

Frei, Hans. *Types of Christian Theology*, eds George Hunsinger and William H. Placher. New Haven, CT: Yale University Press, 1992.

Glasse, John. 'Barth on Feuerbach'. *Harvard Theological Review*, 57, no. 2 (1964), pp. 69–96.

Gould, Stephen Jay. *Rocks of Ages: Science and Religion in the Fulness of Life*. London: Vintage, 2002.

Gould, Stephen Jay and Richard C. Lewontin. 'The Spandrels of San Marco and the Panglossian Paradigm: A Critique of the Adaptationist Programme'. *Proceedings of the Royal Society B* 205 (1979), pp. 581–98.

Gregersen, Niels Henrik. 'Three Varieties of Panentheism'. In Philip Clayton and Arthur Peacocke (eds), *In Whom We Live and Move and Have Our Being: Panentheistic Reflections on God's Presence in a Scientific World*. Grand Rapids, MI: Eerdmans, 2004, pp. 19–35.

Gregersen, Niels Henrik and J. Wentzel van Huyssteen (eds), *Rethinking Theology and Science: Six Models for the Current Dialogue*. Grand Rapids, MI: Eerdmans, 1998.

Griffin, David Ray. 'Panentheism: A Postmodern Revelation'. In Philip Clayton and Arthur Peacocke (eds), *In Whom We Live and Move and Have Our Being: Panentheistic Reflections on God's Presence in a Scientific World*. Grand Rapids, MI: Eerdmans, 2004, pp. 36–47.

Griffin, David Ray. 'Interpreting Science from the Standpoint of Whiteheadian Process Philosophy'. In Philip Clayton (ed.), *The Oxford Handbook of Religion and Science*. Oxford: Oxford University Press, 2008, pp. 453–71.

Harrison, Peter. *The Territories of Science and Religion*. Chicago: University of Chicago Press, 2015.

Hays, Richard B. *The Moral Vision of the New Testament: Community, Cross, New Creation*. San Francisco, CA: HarperSanFrancisco, 1996.

Hefner, Philip. 'Eluding the Chaperones: A Conversation with Phil Hefner, Part II'. *Research News & Opportunities in Science and Theology* 2, no. 2 (October 2001).

Hefner, Philip. 'Religion-and-Science'. In Philip Clayton (ed.), *The Oxford Handbook of Religion and Science*. Oxford: Oxford University Press, 2008, pp. 562–76.

Hoggard Creegan, Nicola. *Animal Suffering and the Problem of Evil*. Oxford: Oxford University Press, 2013.

Hoggard Creegan, Nicola. 'Theodicy: A Response to Christopher Southgate'. *Zygon* 53, no. 3 (2018), pp. 808–20.

Hopkins, Gerard Manley. 'As Kingfishers Catch Fire'. Online at http://www.gutenberg.org/cache/epub/22403/pg22403-images.html.

Hopkins, Gerard Manley. 'That Nature Is a Heraclitean Fire and of the Comfort of the Resurrection'. Online at https://www.poetryfoundation.org/poems/44397/that-nature-is-a-heraclitean-fire-and-of-the-comfort-of-the-resurrection.

Hull, David L. 'The God of the Galápagos'. *Nature* 352 (1991), pp. 485–6.

Huxley, Julian. *Evolution: The Modern Synthesis*. London: Allen and Unwin, 1942.

Kaiser, Christopher. *Creation and the History of Science*. London: Marshall Pickering, 1991.

Katz, Steven T., ed. *Comparative Mysticism: An Anthology of Original Sources*. Oxford: Oxford University Press, 2013.

Kerr, Fergus. *After Aquinas: Versions of Thomism*. Oxford: Blackwell, 2002.

Kingsley, Charles. *The Water-Babies: A Fairy Tale for a Land-Baby*, ed. Brian Alderson. Oxford: Oxford University Press, 2014 [1863].

Knight, Christopher C. *The God of Nature: Incarnation and Contemporary Science*. Minneapolis, MN: Fortress, 2007.

Knight, Christopher C. 'An Eastern Orthodox Critique of the Science-Theology Dialogue.' *Zygon* 51, no. 3 (2016), pp. 573–91.

Laland, Kevin, Tobias Uller, Marc Feldman, Kim Sterelny, Gerd B. Müller, Armin Moczek, Eva Jablonka and John Odling-Smee. 'Does Evolutionary Theory Need a Rethink? Yes, Urgently'. *Nature* 514 (2014), pp. 161–4.

Laland, Kevin, Tobias Uller, Marcus W. Feldman, Kim Sterelny, Gerd B. Müller, Armin Moczek, Eva Jablonka and John Odling-Smee. 'The Extended Evolutionary Synthesis: Its Structure, Assumptions, and Predictions'. *Proceedings of the Royal Society B* 282 (2015), DOI: http://dx.doi.org/10.1098/rspb.2015.1019.

Levy, Neil. 'Analytic and Continental Philosophy: Explaining the Differences'. *Metaphilosophy* 34, no. 3 (2003), pp. 284–304.

Lloyd, Elisabeth. 'Units and Levels of Selection'. In Edward N. Zalta (ed.), *The Stanford Encyclopedia of Philosophy* (Summer 2017 Edition). Online at https://plato.stanford.edu/archives/sum2017/entries/selection-units/.

MacIntyre, Alasdair. *After Virtue: A Study in Moral Theory*, 2nd edn. London: Duckworth, 1985.

MacIntyre, Alasdair. *Whose Justice? Which Rationality?* London: Duckworth, 1988.

McGrath, Alister E. *The Open Secret: A New Vision for Natural Theology*. Oxford: Blackwell, 2008.

McGrath, Alister E. *A Fine-Tuned Universe: The Quest for God in Science and Theology*. Louisville, KY: Westminster John Knox, 2009.

McLeish, Tom. *Faith and Wisdom in Science*. Oxford: Oxford University Press, 2014.

McNamara, Patrick. *The Neuroscience of Religious Experience*. Cambridge: Cambridge University Press, 2009.

Messer, Neil. *Selfish Genes and Christian Ethics: Theological and Ethical Reflections on Evolutionary Biology*. London: SCM, 2007.

Messer, Neil. 'Natural Evil after Darwin'. In Michael Northcott and R. J. Berry (eds), *Theology after Darwin*. Milton Keynes: Paternoster Press, 2009, pp. 139–54.

Messer, Neil. *Theological Neuroethics: Christian Ethics Meets the Science of the Human Brain*. London: Bloomsbury T & T Clark, 2017.

Messer, Neil. 'Evolution and Theodicy: How (Not) to Do Science and Theology'. *Zygon* 53, no. 3 (2018), pp. 821–35.

Messer, Neil. 'Evolution, Animal Suffering and Ethics: A Response to Christopher Southgate'. In Andrew Linzey and Clair Linzey (eds), *The Routledge Handbook of Religion and Animal Ethics*. Abingdon: Routledge, 2018, pp. 337–46.

Meyendorff, John. *Byzantine Theology: Historical Trends and Doctrinal Themes*, 2nd edn. New York: Fordham University Press, 1983.

Moore, Russell D. 'A Creationist Watches Animal Planet™'. *Southern Seminary Magazine*, 74, no. 2 (2006), pp. 10–11.

Morris, Henry M. *Scientific Creationism*, 2nd edn. Green Forest, AR: Master, 1985.

Mühling, Markus. *Resonances: Neurobiology, Evolution and Theology: Evolutionary Niche Construction, the Ecological Brain and Relational-Narrative Theology*. Göttingen: Vandenhoeck & Ruprecht, 2014.

Murphy, Nancey. 'Theology and Science within a Lakatosian Program'. *Zygon* 34, no. 4 (1999), pp. 629–42.

Murphy, Nancey. 'On the Role of Philosophy in Theology-Science Dialogue'. *Theology and Science* 1, no. 1 (2003), pp. 79–93.

Murphy, Nancey. *Bodies and Souls, or Spirited Bodies?*. Cambridge: Cambridge University Press, 2006.

Murphy, Nancey. 'Cognitive Science and the Evolution of Religion: A Philosophical and Theological Appraisal'. In Jeffrey Schloss and Michael J. Murray (eds), *The Believing Primate: Scientific, Philosophical, and Theological Reflections on the Origins of Religion*. Oxford: Oxford University Press, 2009, pp. 265–77.

Murphy, Nancey. 'Avoiding Neurobiological Reductionism'. In Juan José Sanguineti, Aribierto Acerbi and José Angel Lombo (eds), *Moral Behavior and Free Will: A Neurobiological and Philosophical Approach*. Morolo: If Press, 2011, pp. 201–22.

Murphy, Nancey and Warren S. Brown. *Did My Neurons Make Me Do It? Philosophical and Neurobiological Perspectives on Moral Responsibility and Free Will*. Oxford: Oxford University Press, 2007.

Murray, Michael J. and Andrew Goldberg. 'Evolutionary Accounts of Religion: Explaining and Explaining Away'. In Jeffrey Schloss and Michael J. Murray (eds), *The Believing Primate: Scientific, Philosophical, and Theological Reflections on the Origins of Religion*. Oxford: Oxford University Press, 2009, pp. 179–99.

Need, Stephen W. 'Rereading the Prologue: Incarnation and Creation in John 1.1-18'. *Theology* 106 (2003), pp. 397–404.

Newberg, Andrew B. *Principles of Neurotheology*. Farnham: Ashgate, 2010.

Nichols, Ryan and Gideon Yaffe. 'Thomas Reid'. In Edward N. Zalta (ed.), *The Stanford Encyclopedia of Philosophy* (Winter 2016 Edition). Online at https://plato.stanford.edu/archives/win2016/entries/reid/.

Oliver, Simon. 'What Can Theology Offer to Religious Studies?' In Maya Warrier and Simon Oliver (eds), *Theology and Religious Studies: An Exploration of Disciplinary Boundaries*. London: T & T Clark, 2008, pp. 15–29.

Paddison, Angus. *Scripture: A Very Theological Proposal*. London: T & T Clark, 2009.

Paddison, Angus, ed. *Theologians on Scripture*. London: T & T Clark, 2016.

Page, Ruth. *God and the Web of Creation*. London: SCM Press, 1996.

Paley, William. *Natural Theology: Or, Evidences of the Existence and Attributes of the Deity*. London: J. Faulder, 1802.

Papineau, David. 'Naturalism'. In Edward N. Zalta (ed.), *The Stanford Encyclopedia of Philosophy* (Winter 2016 Edition). Online at https://plato.stanford.edu/archives/win2016/entries/naturalism/.

Peacocke, Arthur. *God and the New Biology*. London: Dent and Sons, 1986.

Peacocke, Arthur. *God and Science: A Quest for Christian Credibility*. London: SCM Press, 1996.

Peacocke, Arthur. 'God's Interaction with the World: The Implications of Deterministic "Chaos" and of Interconnected and Interdependent Complexity'. In Robert John Russell, Nancey Murphy and Arthur Peacocke (eds), *Chaos and Complexity: Scientific Perspectives on Divine Action*, 2nd edn. Vatican City: Vatican Observatory/Berkeley, CA: Center for Theology and the Natural Sciences, 1997, pp. 265–87.

Peacocke, Arthur. 'Science and the Future of Theology: Critical Issues'. *Zygon* 35, no. 1 (2000), pp. 119–40.

Peacocke, Arthur. *Paths from Science Towards God: The End of All Our Exploring*. Oxford: Oneworld, 2001.

Peacocke, Arthur. 'The Cost of New Life'. In John Polkinghorne (ed.), *The Work of Love: Creation as Kenosis*. Grand Rapids, MI: Eerdmans, 2001, pp. 21–42.

Perry, John and Sarah Lane Ritchie. 'Magnets, Magic, and Other Anomalies: In Defense of Methodological Naturalism'. *Zygon* 53, no. 4 (2018), pp. 1064–93.

Persinger, Michael A. 'Religious and Mystical Experiences as Artifacts of Temporal Lobe Function: A General Hypothesis'. *Perceptual and Motor Skills* 57 (1983), pp. 1255–62.

Peters, Ted. 'Theology and the Natural Sciences'. In David F. Ford (ed.), *The Modern Theologians*, 2nd edn. Oxford: Blackwell, 1997, pp. 649–67.

Peterson, Gregory R. 'Are Evolutionary/Cognitive Theories of Religion Relevant for Philosophy of Religion?' *Zygon* 45, no. 3 (2010), pp. 545–57.

Phillips, D. Z. *The Problem of Evil and the Problem of God*. London: SCM Press, 2005.

Plantinga, Alvin. 'Games Scientists Play'. In Jeffrey Schloss and Michael J. Murray (eds), *The Believing Primate: Scientific, Philosophical, and*

Theological Reflections on the Origins of Religion. Oxford: Oxford University Press, 2009, pp. 139–67.

Polkinghorne, John. *Science and Christian Belief: Theological Reflections of a Bottom-up Thinker*. London: SPCK, 1994.

Polkinghorne, John. 'The Metaphysics of Divine Action'. In Robert John Russell, Nancey Murphy and Arthur Peacocke (eds), *Chaos and Complexity: Scientific Perspectives on Divine Action*, 2nd edn. Vatican City: Vatican Observatory/Berkeley, CA: Center for Theology and the Natural Sciences, 1997, pp. 147–56.

Polkinghorne, John. *Faith, Science and Understanding*. London: SPCK, 2000.

Polkinghorne, John. *Science and the Trinity: The Christian Encounter with Reality*. London: SPCK, 2004.

Pruss, Alexander R. and Richard M. Gale. 'Cosmological and Design Arguments'. In William J. Wainwright (ed.), *The Oxford Handbook of Philosophy of Religion*. Oxford: Oxford University Press, 2005, pp. 116–37.

Rappaport, Margaret Boone and Christopher Corbally. 'Tracing Origins of Twenty-First Century Ecotheology: The Poetry of Christopher Southgate'. *Zygon* 53, no. 3 (2018), pp. 866–75.

Ritchie, Sarah Lane. 'Dancing Around the Causal Joint: Challenging the Theological Turn in Divine Action Theories'. *Zygon* 52, no. 2 (2017), pp. 361–79.

Ritchie, Sarah Lane. *Divine Action and the Human Mind*. Cambridge: Cambridge University Press, 2019.

Rolston, Holmes III. *Science and Religion: A Critical Survey*. Philadelphia, PA: Templeton Foundation Press, 2006.

Russell, Robert John. 'Divine Action and Quantum Mechanics: A Fresh Assessment'. In Robert John Russell et al. (eds), *Quantum Mechanics: Scientific Perspectives on Divine Action*, 5th ed. Vatican City: Vatican Observatory/Berkeley, CA: Center for Theology and the Natural Sciences, 2002, pp. 293–328.

Russell, Robert John. 'Quantum Theory and the Theology of Non-interventionist Objective Divine Action'. In Philip Clayton (ed.), *The Oxford Handbook of Religion and Science*. Oxford: Oxford University Press, 2008, pp. 579–95.

Russell, Robert John and Kirk Wegter-McNelly. 'Science and Theology: Mutual Interaction'. In Ted Peters and Gaymon Bennett (eds), *Bridging Science and Religion*. London: SCM Press, 2002, pp. 19–34.

Saunders, Nicholas. *Divine Action and Modern Science*. Cambridge: Cambridge University Press, 2002.

Schjoedt, Uffe. 'The Religious Brain: A General Introduction to the Experimental Neuroscience of Religion'. *Method and Theory in the Study of Religion* 21 (2009), pp. 310–39.

Schjoedt, Uffe. 'Does Praying Resemble Normal Interpersonal Interaction?' In D. Jason Slone and William W. McCorkle Jr. (eds), *The Cognitive Science of Religion: A Methodological Introduction to Key Empirical Studies*. London: Bloomsbury, 2019, pp. 203–10.

Schloss, Jeffrey. 'Introduction: Evolutionary Theories of Religion: Science Unfettered or Naturalism Run Wild?' In Jeffrey Schloss and Michael J. Murray (eds), *The Believing Primate: Scientific, Philosophical, and Theological Reflections on the Origins of Religion*. Oxford: Oxford University Press, 2009, pp. 1–25.

Schmemann, Alexander. *The Eucharist: Sacrament of the Kingdom*. Crestwood, NY: St Vladimir's Seminary Press, 1987.

Simon, Pierre (Marquis de Laplace). *A Philosophical Essay on Probabilities*, trans. Frederick Wilson Truscott and Frederick Lincoln Emory. New York: John Wiley, 1902 [1814].

Sorley, W. R. *Moral Values and the Idea of God*. Cambridge: Cambridge University Press, 1919.

Southgate, Christopher. *Easing the Gravity Field: Poems of Science and Love*. Nottingham: Shoestring Press, 2006.

Southgate, Christopher. *The Groaning of Creation: God, Evolution, and the Problem of Evil*. Louisville, KY: Westminster John Knox, 2008.

Southgate, Christopher. 'Re-reading Genesis, John and Job: A Christian Response to Darwinism.' *Zygon* 46, no. 2 (2011), pp. 370–95.

Southgate, Christopher. 'Divine Glory in a Darwinian World'. *Zygon* 49, no. 4 (2014), pp. 784–807.

Southgate, Christopher. 'Does God's Care Make Any Difference?: Theological Reflection on the Suffering of God's Creatures'. In E. M. Conradie, S. Bergmann, C. Deane-Drummond and D. Edwards (eds), *Christian Faith and the Earth: Current Paths and Emerging Horizons in Ecotheology*. London: Bloomsbury, 2014, pp. 97–114.

Southgate, Christopher. 'God's Creation Wild and Violent, and Our Care for Other Animals'. *Perspectives in Science and Christian Faith* 67, no. 4 (2015), pp. 245–53.

Southgate, Christopher. 'Cosmic Evolution and Evil'. In Chad Meister and Paul K. Moser (eds), *The Cambridge Companion to the Problem of Evil*. Cambridge: Cambridge University Press, 2017, pp. 147–64.

Southgate, Christopher. 'Response with a Select Bibliography'. *Zygon* 53, no. 3 (2018), pp. 909–30.

Southgate, Christopher. 'Poetry and Science', unpublished lecture, St Stephen's Church, Exeter, October 2018.

Stenger, Victor J. *God: The Failed Hypothesis – How Science Shows That God Does Not Exist*. Amherst, NY: Prometheus Books, 2007.

Stenger, Victor J. *God and the Folly of Faith: The Incompatibility of Science and Religion*. Amherst, NY: Prometheus Books, 2012.

Stenger, Victor J. *God and the Atom*. Amherst, NY: Prometheus Books, 2013.

Stenger, Victor J. *God and the Universe*. Amherst, NY: Prometheus Books, 2014.

Stenmark, Lisa L. 'Going Public: Feminist Epistemologies, Hannah Arendt, and the Science-and-Religion Discourse'. In Philip Clayton (ed.), *The Oxford Handbook of Religion and Science*. Oxford: Oxford University Press, 2008, pp. 821–34.

Stenmark, Mikael. 'Ways of Relating Science and Religion'. In Peter Harrison (ed.), *The Cambridge Companion to Science and Religion*. Cambridge: Cambridge University Press, 2010, pp. 278–95.

Stoeger, William R. 'Describing God's Action in the World in Light of Scientific Knowledge of Reality'. In Robert John Russell, Nancey Murphy and Arthur Peacocke (eds), *Chaos and Complexity: Scientific Perspectives on Divine Action*, 2nd edn. Vatican City: Vatican Observatory/Berkeley, CA: Center for Theology and the Natural Sciences, 1997, pp. 239–61.

Stoeger, William R. 'Contemporary Physics and the Ontological Status of the Laws of Nature'. In Robert John Russell, Nancey Murphy and C. J. Isham (eds), *Quantum Cosmology and the Laws of Nature: Scientific Perspectives on Divine Action*, 2nd edn. Vatican City: Vatican Observatory/Berkeley, CA: Center for Theology and the Natural Sciences, 1999, pp. 207–31.

Stoeger, William R. 'The Divine Action Project: Reflections on the Compatibilism/Incompatibilism Divide'. *Theology and Science* 2, no. 2 (2004), pp. 192–6.

Stoeger, William R. 'Conceiving Divine Action in a Dynamic Universe'. In Robert John Russell, Nancey Murphy and William R. Stoeger (eds), *Scientific Perspectives on Divine Action: Twenty Years of Challenge and Progress*. Vatican City: Vatican Observatory/Berkeley, CA: Center for Theology and the Natural Sciences, 2008, pp. 225–47.

Stout, Jeffrey. *Ethics after Babel: The Languages of Morals and Their Discontents*. Boston: Beacon Press, 1988.

St-Pierre, L. S. and M. A. Persinger. 'Experimental Facilitation of the Sensed Presence Is Predicted by the Specific Patterns of the Applied Magnetic Fields, Not by Suggestibility: Re-analyses of 19 Experiments'. *International Journal of Neuroscience* 116 (2006), pp. 1079–96.

Swinton, John. *Raging with Compassion: Pastoral Responses to the Problem of Evil*. Grand Rapids: Eerdmans, 2007.

Temple, Frederick. *The Relations between Religion and Science: Eight Lectures Preached before the University of Oxford in the Year 1884*. London: Macmillan, 1884. Online at http://anglicanhistory.org/eng land/ftemple/bampton/

Thomas Aquinas. *Summa Theologiae*, trans. Fathers of the English Dominican Province, 2nd edn. (1920). Online at http://www.newa dvent.org/summa/index.html.

Thomas, R. S. *Collected Poems 1945–1990*. London: J.M. Dent, 1993.

Thomas, R. S. *Autobiographies*, trans. Jason Walford Davies. London: Phoenix, 1997.

Thomas, R. S. *Selected Poems*. London: Penguin, 2003.

Torrance, Andrew B. 'Should a Christian Accept Methodological Naturalism?' *Zygon* 52, no. 3 (2017), pp. 691–725.

Torrance, Andrew B. 'The Possibility of a Theology-Engaged Science: A Response to Perry and Ritchie'. *Zygon* 53, no. 4 (2018), pp. 1094–105.

Tyrrell, George. *Through Scylla and Charibdis, or the Old Theology and the New*. London: Longmans, Green and Co., 1907.

Van Slyke, James A. 'Challenging the By-Product Theory of Religion in the Cognitive Science of Religion'. *Theology and Science* 8, no. 2 (2010), pp. 163–80.

Vogel, Manfred H. 'The Barth-Feuerbach Confrontation'. *Harvard Theological Review* 59, no. 1 (1966), pp. 27–52.

Warrier, Maya and Simon Oliver, eds *Theology and Religious Studies: An Exploration of Disciplinary Boundaries* (London: T & T Clark, 2008).

Welker, Michael. 'Science and Theology: Their Relation at the Beginning of the Third Millenium [*sic*]'. In Philip Clayton (ed.), *The Oxford Handbook of Religion and Science*. Oxford: Oxford University Press, 2008, pp. 551–61.

Whitehead, Alfred North. *Process and Reality*, eds David Ray Griffin and Donald W. Sherburne. New York: Free Press, 1978.

Wildman, Wesley J. 'The Divine Action Project, 1988–2003'. *Theology and Science* 2, no. 1 (2004), pp. 31–75.

Wildman, Wesley J. 'Incongruous Goodness, Perilous Beauty, Disconcerting Truth: Ultimate Reality and Suffering in Nature'. In Nancey Murphy, Robert John Russell and William R. Stoeger (eds), *Physics and Cosmology: Scientific Perspectives on the Problem of Natural Evil*. Vatican City: Vatican Observatory/Berkeley, CA: Center for Theology and the Natural Sciences, 2007, pp. 267–94.

Wildman, Wesley J. *In Our Own Image: Anthropomorphism, Apophaticism, and Ultimacy*. Oxford: Oxford University Press, 2017.

Williams, Thomas. 'Saint Anselm'. In Edward N. Zalta (ed.), *The Stanford Encyclopedia of Philosophy* (Spring 2016 Edition). Online at https://pl ato.stanford.edu/archives/spr2016/entries/anselm/.

Wilson, David Sloan. *Darwin's Cathedral: Evolution, Religion, and the Nature of Society*. Chicago, IL: University of Chicago Press, 2002.

Wilson, David Sloan. 'Evolutionary Social Constructivism: Narrowing (but Not Yet Bridging) the Gap'. In Jeffrey Schloss and Michael J.

Murray (eds), *The Believing Primate: Scientific, Philosophical, and Theological Reflections on the Origins of Religion*. Oxford: Oxford University Press, 2009, pp. 319–38.

Wilson, David Sloan and Elliott Sober. 'Reintroducing Group Selection to the Human Behavioral Sciences'. *Behavioral and Brain Sciences* 7, no. 4 (1994), pp. 585–654.

Wray, Gregory A., Hopi E. Hoekstra, Douglas J. Futuyma, Richard E. Lenski, Trudy F. C. Mackay, Dolph Schluter and Joan E. Strassmann. 'Does Evolutionary Theory Need a Rethink? No, All Is Well'. *Nature* 514 (2014), pp. 161, 163–4.

Wright, John, ed. *Postliberal Theology and the Church Catholic: Conversations with George Lindbeck, David Burrell, and Stanley Hauerwas*. Grand Rapids, MI: Baker Academic, 2012.

Yong, Amos. *The Spirit of Creation: Modern Science and Divine Action in the Pentecostal-Charismatic Imagination*. Grand Rapids, MI: Eerdmans, 2011.

INDEX